SECRET PROJECTS OF THE
KRIEGSMARINE

SECRET PROJECTS OF THE KRIEGSMARINE

UNSEEN DESIGNS OF NAZI GERMANY'S NAVY

NICO SGARLATO
ALESSIO SGARLATO

Greenhill Books

Secret Projects of the Kriegsmarine
First published in English in 2022 by
Greenhill Books,
c/o Pen & Sword Books Ltd,
47 Church Street, Barnsley,
S. Yorkshire, S70 2AS

www.greenhillbooks.com
contact@greenhillbooks.com

Published and distributed in the United States of America and Canada
by the Naval Institute Press, 291 Wood Road, Annapolis,
Maryland 21402-5043

www.usni.org

ISBN: 978–1–78438–687–0

All rights reserved.

First published in Italian as
I Progetti Segreti della Kriegsmarine
© Delta Editrice 2017

This English-language edition © Greenhill Books 2022

The rights of Nico Sgarlatto and Alessio Sgarlato to be identified as authors of this work have been asserted in accordance with Section 77 of the Copyrights Designs and Patents Act 1988.

CIP data records for this title are available from the British Library

Designed and typeset by Donald Sommerville

Printed and bound in the UK
by CPI Group (UK) Ltd, Croydon, CR0 4YY

Typeset in 11/15 pt Adobe Caslon Pro

Contents

	Introduction	vii
PART I	*Secret Underwater Weapons*	1
PART II	*Piloted Torpedoes and Midget Submarines*	52
PART III	*Major Surface Vessels*	105
PART IV	*Smaller Surface Vessels*	143
PART V	*Landing Wonder Weapons*	162
	Select Bibliography	182

Introduction

It is undeniable that in the history of nations there are very specific turning points that shape their future actions and therefore their destiny. In the case of Germany, the series of events that led to the outbreak of the Second World War in Europe could arguably have been stimulated by two fundamental aspects: the consequences of the Treaty of Versailles which, following defeat during the First World War, had placed severe limits on military activities and, secondly, the natural German inclination for technological sophistication that was generally superior to the average 'state of the art' within other industrialised countries.

Thus, to take perhaps the most obvious example, the prohibition of building conventional military aircraft led to greater interest in training with gliders that resulted in superior knowledge in the field of aerodynamics and an accompanying search for non-traditional means of propulsion. These could be seen to culminate in the cutting-edge results in the fields of rockets and jet aircraft.

However, clarity of vision did not always accompany such achievements in a nation where 'personality politics' frequently overruled military sense. For example, despite the enormous industrial potential that allowed high levels of production of fighter planes and armoured vehicles, the untimely pre-war death of a single Luftwaffe tactician (Generalleutnant Walther Wever) resulted in the German war machine paying scant attention to the potential role of strategic heavy bombers; aircraft such as the American B-17, B-24 and B-29 or the British Avro Lancaster, all of which played a fundamental part in the victory of the Allies.

Germany never possessed a navy comparable in size to those of Japan, Great Britain, Italy and the United States. An aim for parity with the French Navy could never be achieved and, despite early mistaken beliefs that 'cruiser warfare' by means of capital ships against British supply and trade lines would be possible for the Kriegsmarine, the disappointing use of what battleships and heavy cruisers the Germans did possess led, eventually, to the Kriegsmarine staking any chance of victory on U-boats.

These underwater units, the famous U-boats, achieved a certain level of success, particularly against Allied merchant traffic but also periodically against British warships, perhaps most notably in the Mediterranean Sea. Though the U-boat service had been starved of resources so long that it never truly stood a chance of reaching the heights achieved by its forebears of the previous war, the U-boat success that had been achieved led to studies of other types of underwater vehicles, trailing in the wake of what had already been done by Germany's Axis partners Japan and Italy.

Unlike in Italy, where small coastal submarines were built in limited numbers and where assault vehicles equipped a single unit, the Kriegsmarine (as well as the Imperial Japanese Navy) later attempted to mass-produce these types of craft, though they were only ever capable of a minor contribution to German naval operations; indisputably the most successful were Germany's midget submarines.

The underlying German desire for the maximum exploitation of technology also led to the creation of hybrid systems, able to move independently on land, the sea surface or underwater.

When it comes to German 'secret weapons' or 'secret projects' it seems that no one can claim to have covered the subject exhaustively. This text focuses on submarines and unconventional surface boats as well as on projects that the Kriegsmarine never fully developed; Germany's experiments with armaments, propulsion, detection equipment and more lie outside the scope of this study.

The authors would like to thank Giorgio Tanzi for the advice provided regarding the aircraft embarked on submarines.

Franco Harrauer (1927–2016)

The naval architect Franco Harrauer made this book possible due to his extensive research into unconventional German naval units, combined with his pleasant descriptive style and an extraordinary skill in drawing. By profession he was a designer of pleasure boats – both sailing and motorboats – often in collaboration with Renato (Sonny) Levi, showing a particular propensity for catamarans. Harrauer drew on typical aeronautical construction solutions for the Tiger Shark family of light alloy hulls but also designed iron ships and patented some devices, such as retractable rudders and the entire design of a fast amphibious craft.

He worked in Italy and elsewhere, mainly in Egypt and Brazil, spending a major part of his life in the latter. He also wrote extensively for the magazine *Eserciti nella Storia* ('Armies in History') and for the Internet site *'AltoMareBlu'* (Blue High Seas), proving his skills as a writer and providing an important contribution to the knowledge of certain topics such as, for example, Italian assault vehicles. His role in bringing this information to light was so valuable that it can be said, without fear of denial, that without his work a piece of history would have been lost.

PART I

Secret Underwater Weapons

The submarine retained an important position in the field of inter-war German technological research, although its true potential may not have been appreciated in the lead-up to war and even in its early stages. The Kriegsmarine General Staff (OKM) retained an obsession with large surface fleets, mistakenly believing that traditional ideas of 'cruiser warfare' against enemy supply lines would lead to victory and harbouring an unrealistic aim to create a balanced fleet capable of contesting the established might of the Royal Navy. This belief was no doubt heavily underpinned by Adolf Hitler's pledge that his navy would not need to fight a war before 1948, theoretically allowing time for an ambitious construction plan, though limited resources which all branches of Germany's armed services were competing for would never have allowed it to reach fruition.

There were, however, visionaries within the Kriegsmarine who did truly see the potential and strategic usefulness of a variety of underwater weapons. Karl Dönitz became the head of the fledgling U-boat force in 1936, though he initially exercised no control over construction and development of the U-boat; his remit remained tactical. Conventional U-boats remained firmly based on 'tried and tested' First World War designs, rather than embracing radical new technologies that were already on offer within Germany. Backing for such ideas was – as in matters of aerial warfare – was only fully provided once the war had already started to go against Germany. Nevertheless, in limited ways, such projects had been established by the outbreak of war by men who had already begun technological engineering studies that could be shaped for military purposes; this had been a sure way to obtain funding as Germany rearmed and built the Wehrmacht into a premier fighting force.

Such experimental projects in the field of underwater technology followed three main threads: to obtain ever faster vessels, particularly with high underwater speed; to create hybrid boats that combined capabilities similar to those of surface vehicles while retaining the ability to dive; and to design and construct completely new and unconventional units.

The Walter Submarines
(*V-80*, Type XVII and *Schwertwal*)

Hellmuth Walter's projects are some of the boldest experiments in the first of the three fields just mentioned: obtaining ever faster speeds underwater. Born in Wedel, Schleswig-Holstein, in 1900, Walter had trained to become a machinist during the time of the First World War. In 1921 he began studies in mechanical engineering at the Technical University of Berlin, leaving to take up a position with the Stettiner Maschinenbau AG 'Vulcan' shipyard before he had completed his studies. There he worked on gas turbine designs and developed a strong interest in overcoming limitations in underwater machinery imposed by the internal combustion engine. His reasoning centred on the possibility that an engine powered by a fuel source already rich in oxygen would not require external oxygen and, therefore, could operate efficiently while submerged. In 1925 he patented his idea that hydrogen peroxide (H_2O_2) could be a suitable fuel; once a suitable permanganate catalyst was introduced the fuel would break down to superheated steam at over 500 °C and oxygen, its heat causing expansion and therefore becoming a source of pressure. By the introduction of diesel fuel into this mixture, combustion could be triggered which would provide increased power potential and drive a high-speed turbine. The exhaust and condensed steam would then be expelled overboard.

In 1933, Walter transferred to Friedrich Krupp's Germaniawerft shipyard in Kiel – once a major builder of U-boats during the First World War and soon to become the same during the

The 76-ton Walter *V-80* midget submarine during a sea trial carried out in the spring of 1940 in the waters off Kiel where it was built.

Second. There he experimented with an innovative naval propulsion system: a turbine driven by the reaction between hydrogen peroxide (Walter claiming to use a 'stabilised formula') and a petroleum-based oxidiser. His goal was to obtain a lighter submarine engine than any currently in existence. In 1934 he formalised his project in a proposal for the Reich War Ministry (forerunner of the Oberkommando der Wehrmacht, which was created in 1938) for the construction of a submarine with a displacement of only 300 tons, that is more or less like a coastal unit, but capable of travelling at 26 knots on the surface and reaching the unprecedented speed of 30 knots in depth. By way of comparison, the conventional Type II U-boat developed in secret in Finland and about to begin construction in Germany, travelled at maximum speeds of 7 knots submerged and 13 knots surfaced.

However, because the Kriegsmarine's strategy at that time emphasised surface ships, the proposal was not taken seriously and remained in limbo until 1937. During that year, Walter managed to attract the attention of Karl Dönitz, at that point a *Kapitän zur See* in command of the small U-boat service and directly responsible for the training of future submariners. Two years later, in 1939, Dönitz managed to obtain a contract for Walter for the construction of

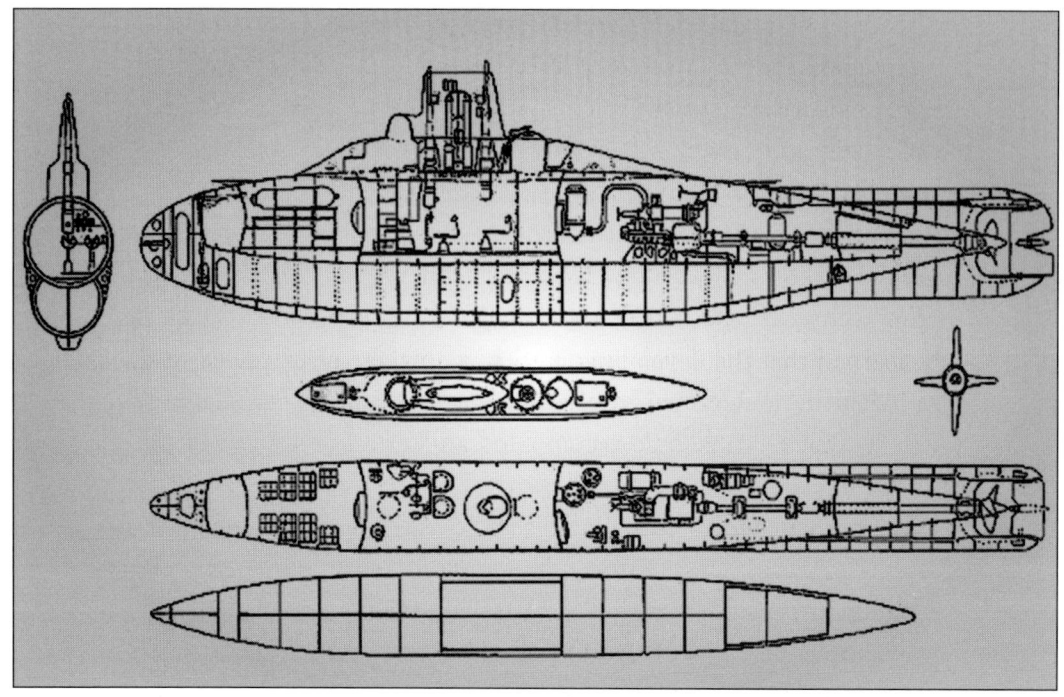

Sectional drawings of the Walter *V-80*.

an experimental vessel, or as we would say today, a demonstration prototype, based on his revolutionary idea. This vessel was given the designation *V-80*.

On 14 April 1940, while the Kriegsmarine was elsewhere heavily involved in the invasion of Norway, *V-80* (displacement 76 tons, length 22 metres) left a slipway of Kiel's Germaniawerft under absolute secrecy and was put through a series of tests, usually under Walter's direct control as one of the four-man crew, alongside his test engineer Heinz Ullrich. Results were extremely positive, with a maximum underwater speed recorded off Hela in the Gulf of Danzig of 28.1 knots: not as high as theoretically projected, but nonetheless a result that far outclassed any existing submarine technology. Carried by a renewed wave of enthusiasm, Germany's decision-makers ordered the immediate construction of six coastal vessels that displayed the same characteristics as the prototype. However, with the placing of this order, controversy arose from an unexpected direction. Dönitz's U-boats were struggling at sea with inefficient weaponry – the disastrous torpedo crisis that drew the U-boats' teeth – and a dearth of available boats, as deliveries never kept pace with expectation. Germany's shipyards and construction manpower were stretched to capacity and beyond, a situation made worse by heavy combat losses suffered during the Norwegian campaign. Dönitz needed U-boats at sea now. In a Paris conference with Walter and other technical experts from the Kriegsmarine's construction branch, he learned that the developing craft was nowhere near service-ready as it had been sidelined by the hard-pressed shipyards. There was no way that Dönitz could recommend any kind of mass production for an unproven design and *V-80* was, in any event, too small for effective tactics to be formulated that could exploit the possibilities of this extraordinary vehicle. Dönitz therefore requested that the production capacities of the German shipyards be reserved for the conventional Types VII and IX, of which he felt a more immediate need. However, this same conference also yielded impetus for the development of a U-boat using Walter's streamlined hull-form with vastly increased battery capacity, thereby going some way to satisfying the demand for a '100 per cent underwater vehicle'. This idea would later yield the Type XXI and Type XXIII 'electro-boats': vast improvements on current U-boat types. Furthermore Walter suggested the creation of a retractable ventilation apparatus that could allow existing diesel boats to run their engines and recharge batteries while remaining submerged, dovetailing with technology already under development by the Dutch Navy since 1933. From this would emerge the '*Schnorchel*' (snorkel) which prolonged the operational life of the Type VII and Type IX U-boats.

Walter then tried the path of compromise by beginning the design of a larger 655-ton submarine using the same propulsion technology and armed with six torpedo tubes; *V-300* (later called Type XVII, *U-791*) which for a displacement of 600 tons expected to obtain a submerged speed of 19 knots, manned by a crew of twenty-five men. However, the vessel never got further than initial planning as immediate variations were introduced and the single prototype

Type XVIIB U-boat.

design was instead changed to models being constructed by two source yards, both capitalising on their own established experience of building U-boats. The new design's range was increased and the Walter peroxide turbines upgraded.

After a meeting with Dönitz, contracts were signed in January 1942 for four Type XVIIA units to be built: order Wk202 (*U-792* and *U-793*) at the Blohm & Voss shipyard in Hamburg and order Wa201 (*U-794* and *U-795*) at Kiel's Germaniawerft. The Hamburg keels were laid in December 1942, those in Kiel following suit in February 1943. The first to carry out water tests was *U-792*, launched on 28 September 1943, soon joined by *U-794*, launched in Kiel on 7 October 1943. The two were used thereafter as experimental and training units and during test runs later in 1944 reached a submerged speed of 25 knots. During a demonstration carried out by *U-794* in the Bay of Danzig in March 1944, Dönitz and four other admirals personally witnessed the U-boat achieve a submerged speed of 24 knots.

In late 1942 Walter proposed a project for a 1,475-ton U-boat – the Type XVIII – capable of carrying 23 torpedoes and on 4 January 1943 contracts for the construction of two examples designated *U-796* and *U-797* were approved for Deutsche Werke in Kiel. However, after the two had been transferred to Germaniwerft for completion in December 1943, they were both cancelled on 28 March 1944 in favour of the Type XXI, with diesel-electric propulsion, increased battery capacity and derived from the hydrodynamic hull-shape of Walter's models. These were considered an improvement of existing designs, rather than new technology, and therefore presented a lower development risk, and could reach 17 knots under water.

The limited consideration of Walter's creations was not, however, entirely unjustified: his projects required difficult construction techniques to extremely high tolerances and demanded complex maintenance once built. Furthermore, they were powered by a fuel both highly flammable and difficult to obtain. When, after the war, the British were able to examine the existing Walter U-boats they were again deemed of little interest.

Although Walter submarines never participated in operational activity, three Type XVIIB units built by the Blohm & Voss shipyard in Hamburg were designed for entry into service: *U-1405*, *U-1406* and *U-1407*. The first of these was used as a training vessel after being commissioned into the Kriegsmarine on 21 December 1944, scuttled in Eckernfjörde Bay on 5 May and the wreck later broken up. The other two were commissioned in February and March 1945 respectively and both surrendered on 5 May in Cuxhaven. However, after both crews had been removed and placed in a prisoner of war camp, the two U-boats were moored alongside a German Vorpostenboot guard ship *V-1267* when Oberleutnant (Ing.) Gerhard Grumpelt, not a member of either crew but a member of the U-boat Technical Training Group and held temporarily aboard the guard ship, boarded both boats and opened their main vents and flooding valves to scuttle them as a belated part of Operation 'Regenbogen'; the plan for self-destruction of the German underwater fleet that had been drawn up as an alternative to

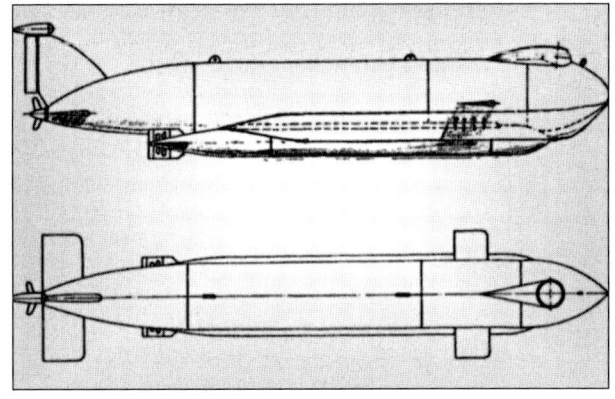

The initial *Schwertwal I* design.

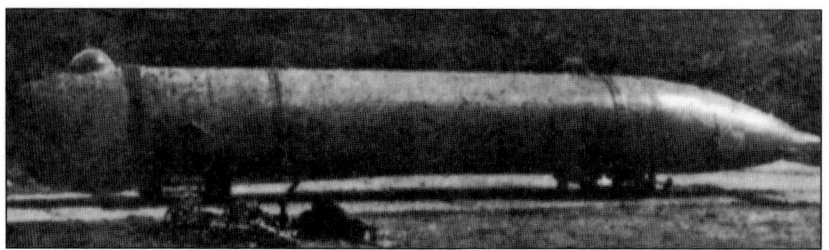

The prototype of the *Schwertwal*, ready to start static tests though its keel has not yet been fitted.

its requisition by the Allies. Grumpelt was court-martialled by the British military for what it regarded as a 'war crime' and received a seven-year prison sentence (subsequently reduced to five).

U-1406 was later raised, taken to the USA aboard the transport ship USS *Shoemaker* and used in trials by the US Navy until scrapped in 1948. *U-1407* was also raised and taken as a prize by the Royal Navy, eventually becoming the test submarine HMS *Meteorite* and carrying out trials, under the guidance of Professor Walter himself and his original team, until being scrapped in 1949. Though capable of impressive speeds, *Meteorite* was unpopular with its crew who regarded it as volatile and difficult to handle underwater; the boat and its machinery were also officially described by the Royal Navy as '75 per cent safe'.

Walter turbines had also been tested by the Kriegsmarine on another prototype; the *Schwertwal* ('Orca'). This midget submarine resembled the Japanese *Kaiten* piloted torpedo. An 800-hp Walter turbine guaranteed it exceptional performance capability and it carried a formidable payload in the shape of

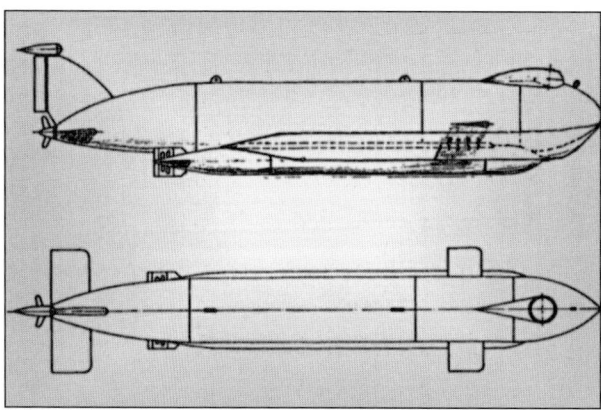

The initial *Schwertwal 1* design. A *Schwertwal 2* was also considered with more hydrodynamic lines; however, it did not pass the stage of preliminary drawings.

either a 500-kg mine or, according to Franco, two G7e electric torpedoes.

The *Schwertal* hull form was tested in the aero-hydrodynamic gallery of the Brunswick Research Institute. The pilot's capabilities were extremely limited; at the speed he moved a periscope was deemed completely useless, so the only direct vision system he possessed was a transparent dome over his seat. Plans were made to install a detection and navigation system with a Patin directional gyro as well as an autopilot. A gyro-stabilised Askania compass of aeronautical origin was installed at the upper end of the centreboard, separate from the metal mass of either the hull and engine, acting as an automatic control of lateral movement and depth. The *Schwertwal* was launched in time to take part in some fairly successful trials in April 1945 and reached almost 35 knots, before the end of the war resulted in it being scuttled in Lake Plön, near the Walter workshops. Harrauer describes the engine of this underwater weapon as follows:

A scale model of *Schwertwal I*; only the prototype was actually built.

> a turbine of 500 hp, later raised to 800 hp, running on Ingolin, a fuel based on hydrogen peroxide which reacted with a hydrazine hydrate based comburent and methanol; therefore an internal combustion and closed-cycle engine that left behind only a trail of water emulsified by high temperature steam ... The vapour trail was due to the exhaust of the turbine which used sea water in an open circuit. This type of steam turbine, at the expense of the life of the engine, was subject to severe corrosion and sodium chloride encrustations, but could do without complicated and heavy condensers for the recovery of water and the related tanks.

KEY TO CROSS SECTION OF SCHWERTWAL
1. Pilot
2. Perspex cupola
3. Second crewman
4. Compensating tank
5. Comburent tank (1 ton)
6. Command transmitter
7. Ingolin fuel tank (10 tons)
8. Gyroscopically stabilised master compass
9. Contra-rotating propellers
10. Walter turbine
11. Compressed air tank
12. G7e torpedo

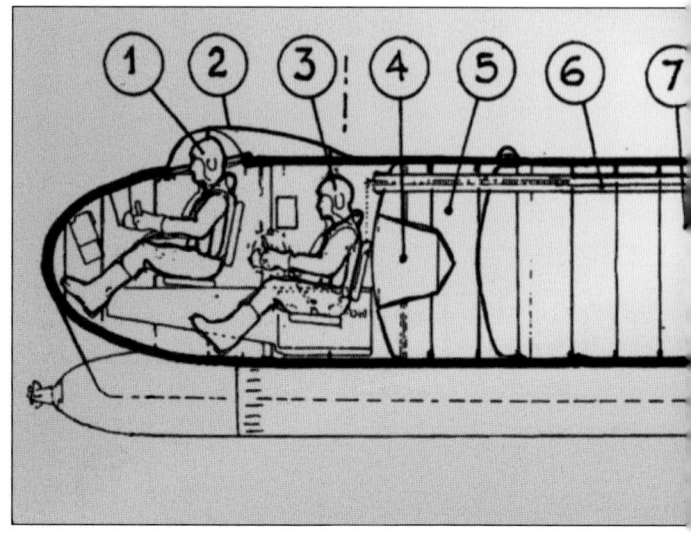

This great historian of such unconventional boats compares the bizarre device to a fighter aircraft, for the speed and combat capability it could have demonstrated. Noting that its range could not have exceeded 100 miles, he hypothesises that it probably would have been carried into action aboard a mother submarine, or via an S-boat (*Schnellboot*) equipped with launch rails. There was also a further proposal for a more streamlined and lighter *Schwertwal 2* that never left the drawing board. With its distant Japanese relative, the *Schwertwal* shared a gloomy design characteristic: though it resembled the Japanese suicide weapon, the two crewmen were theoretically capable of being recovered, but, in reality, the speed of navigation and control difficulties would have created huge problems if the vessel needed to be abandoned and would almost certainly have resulted in the two-man crew's death.

The Schertel-Sachsenberg Submersible Hydrofoil

Technological research and military developments usually work hand in hand, even when the latter does not lead the former. The use for military purposes or the integration of any invention in the field of transport into weapon systems is a trend that has been repeated in every conflict; Germany was not the only nation to experiment boldly with transport designs which would be co-opted by the

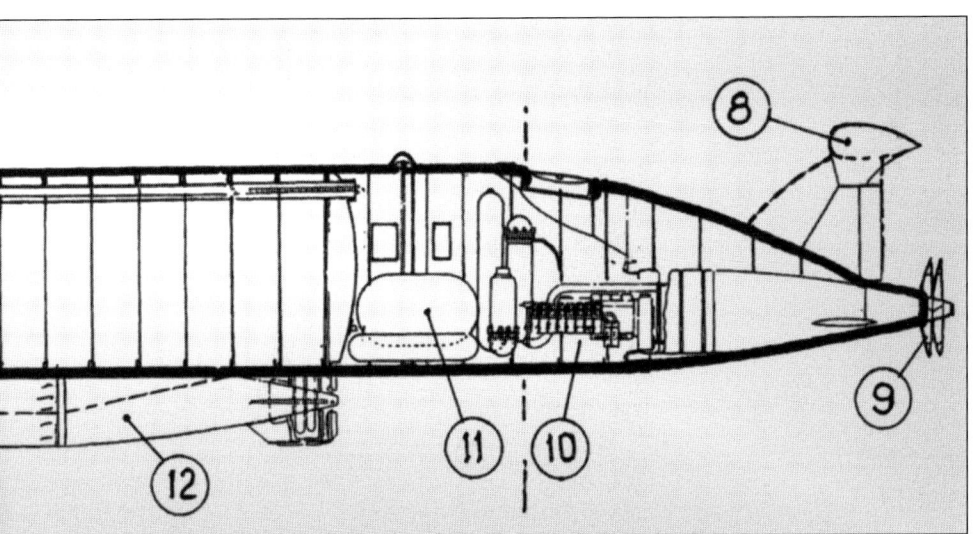

military. One such creation was Schertel and Sachsenberg's attempt to unite in a single vessel both the submarine and the hydrofoil.

The first attempts to build a boat capable of navigating by hydrodynamic support – that is, thanks to pressure on the external surface of a foil immersed in the water, and not by the displacement pressure on the bottom of a hull – took place in the early 1900s. Its pioneers were the inventors and aviation pioneers Brazilian Alberto Santos-Dumont, American Graham Bell and the Italians Arturo Crocco, Ottavio Ricaldoni and Enrico Forlanini. Santos-Dumont built a boat that already had many similarities to a modern hydrofoil but which sank sensationally in the River Seine, probably because he had not considered the reaction torque of the aircraft propeller he

VS-5 (Schertel-Sachsenberg) Technical Details	
Displacement:	between 105 and 120 tons
Length:	25.30 metres (other sources say 34.50 metres)
Beam:	6.60 metres
Propulsion:	2 × Mercedes-Benz MB 501 diesel engines, total 2,500 hp; + one electric motor
Speed:	42 knots (78 km/h) surface; 5 kt (9.25 km/h) underwater
Armament:	2 × 533-mm torpedoes, 1 × 20-mm Mauser *Vierling* installation

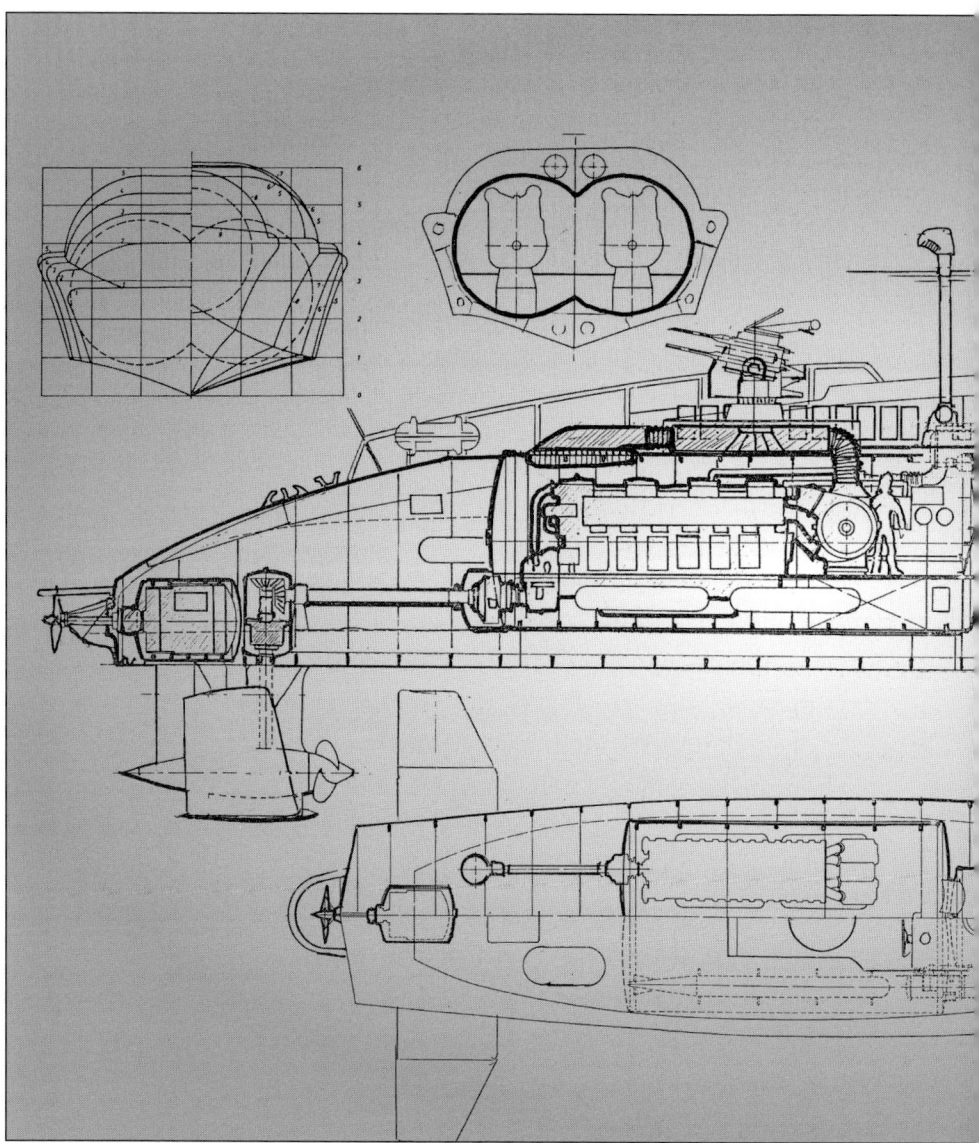

had installed. Forlanini was the first to file patents for a similar vessel in Britain and America, while Crocco and Ricaldoni built and tested the first 'hydroplane', still visible today in the Italian Air Force Museum at Vigna di Valle on Lake Bracciano.

In 1927, the researches of these brilliant engineers which had also been advanced by Bell with the help of experienced naval technicians such as Casey Baldwin and John Thornycroft, were further developed

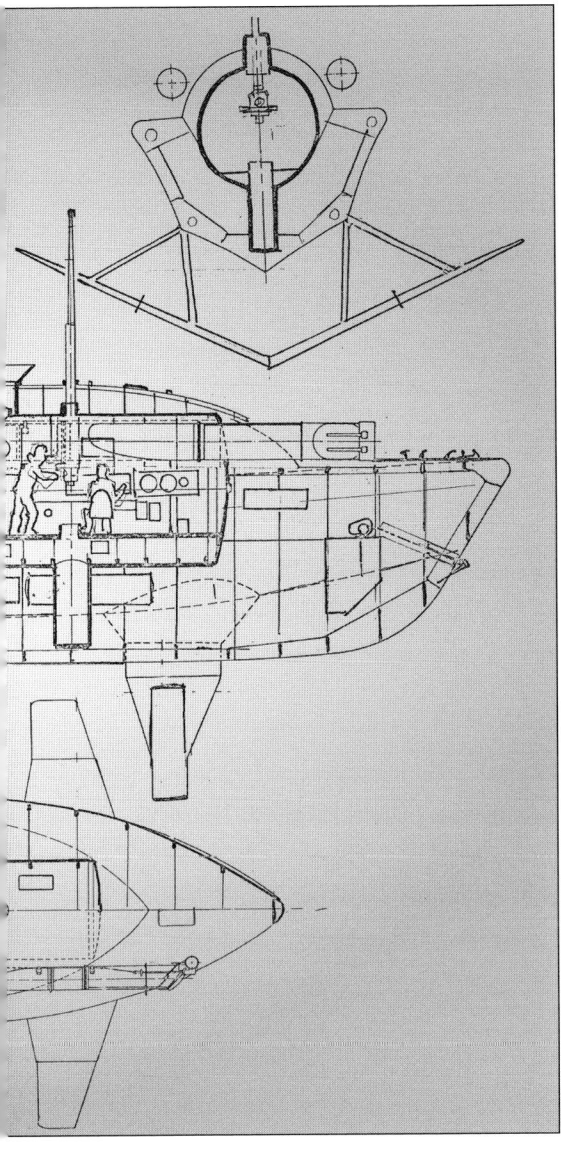

Sectional views of the Schertel-Sachsenberg planned 105-ton submersible motor torpedo boat hydrofoil.

by Baron Hanns von Schertel, then twenty-five years old, who had renewed Forlanini's expired Italian patent in his own name. By 1937, Schertel had experimented at the University of Berlin with tank simulations of as many as seventeen different hydrofoil models, but all characterised by the self-stabilising semi-submerged geometric wing in tandem configuration. In 1939 the Kriegsmarine commissioned a series of tests in the waters of the Baltic Sea of a hydrofoil designed by Schertel from the Gebrüder Sachsenberg shipyard in Dessau-Rosslau. From these experiments came a prototype hydrofoil S-boat intended for use as a coastal minesweeper with the particular intention of patrolling Norwegian fjords; the *VS-1* to *VS-6* series was built by Deschimag in Bremen. Originally, the vessels had been designated TS – *Tragflügel Schnellboot* (Hydrofoil Speedboat) – though this was adapted to VS, standing instead for *Versuchs Schnellboot* (Experimental Speedboat). These vessels, built with heavy materials such as steel, were about 17 knots faster than any traditional hulled coastal unit and had fins equipped with flaps, which allowed them to counteract

The *Schell I* hydrofoil under construction in the Sachsenberg yard in 1941. This transport design seems to have been begun following an Army request during the abortive preparations for the invasion of England in 1940.

the roll and pitch caused by heavy seas. Still incorporated in the hydrofoils of today, these functions follow the principles established by Schertel but are now completely automated.

The speed of 47 knots that *VS-6* reached so impressed the German Navy that it issued an order for a series of thirty-six hydrofoils to be used as fast 6-ton patrol boats, characterised by the novelty of a fixed stern drive with counter-rotating propellers. They were built with 11-mm steel hulls and equipped with 380-hp Lorraine-Dietrich engines.

However, the original order was modified to just six, each displacing 4.9 tons empty or 6.3 tons under load. Measuring 11.96 metres in length they had a beam of 2.7 metres and draught at slow speed of 1.7 metres, reduced to 85 cm when planing on hydrofoils. Armed with a Luftwaffe 15-mm machine gun in an enclosed turret behind the bridge, the boats were manned by a crew of four. The final boat of the series, *VS-6*, was not finished until immediately before the war's end as OKM had asked for it to be redesigned as a fast minelayer capable of carrying four TMB mines. It was seized by Russian forces after the German surrender and subsequently underwent performance tests on the Volga.

In 1941 a motor torpedo version was derived from this project, which was named *VS-7*. Armed with two torpedo tubes and an automatic turreted cannon, this new vessel was powered by a 675-hp Avia engine and could achieve 54 knots. However, by the time that the prototype was ready for operational tests, the British and American navies had already launched motor torpedo boats which operated at an effective speed greater than 30 knots and, even without the dizzying performance of hydrofoils, possessed excellent stability and fighting power. Therefore, the *VS-7* project was stopped.

Schertel's most memorable designs, however, was the *VS-8*. During 1941, as the war in North Africa escalated, both the Italian and German military were searching for methods by which supplies could be rapidly transported to Axis forces there through the Sicilian channel without falling prey to the increasingly active Allied naval and aerial forces in the Mediterranean thanks to British control of the island of Malta. Italian convoys had been systematically ambushed by British forces and the shortage of material quickly inhibited the war of movement at that tme under way in Libya. To cross these treacherous waters quickly, OKW commissioned an 80-ton hydrofoil from the Sachsenberg shipyards, capable of a speed of over 40 knots, capable of carrying a tank of up to 30 tons weight or an equivalent load and ideally able to undertake such operations under cover of the hours of darkness. The major difficulty facing this project was the creation of a rapid disembarkation system that could be used on sloping beaches. Therefore, a stern that resembled a floating dock

VS-8 Technical Details	
Displacement:	80 tons
Length:	32 metres
Propulsion:	2 × Mercedes-Benz diesel engines, total 500 hp.
Speed:	37–40 knots (68.5–74 km/h)
Armament:	2 × 533-mm G7e torpedoes

was designed, capable of releasing a light alloy, motorised landing barge into the sea which could carry the payload ashore. The release of this barge was made possible by lowering the level to which the hydrofoils were submerged thanks to a floodable double-bottomed hull.

However, despite its impetus being the struggle in North Africa, not until August 1943, after the surrender of the last remaining Axis forces penned in Tunisia, did *VS-8* undergo trials in which it performed very well. With an engine that was 24 per cent less powerful than that specified in the original design, it still managed to reach the required 40 knots in calm sea. In seas with waves up to 180 cm high (just above Beaufort Scale 4 weather) it could travel at 37 knots. The hydrofoil S-boat was 31.9 metres long, built entirely in light alloy and powered by two supercharged 20-cylinder Daimler-Benz MB 501 engines that produced 500 hp. The craft's beam was 8 metres for the hull and 10.62 metres at the hydrofoils; the draught at low speeds was 4.25 metres and 2 metres when moving at speed.

VS-8 (ex-Schell I) in harbour. The cargo deck at the stern is clearly shown.

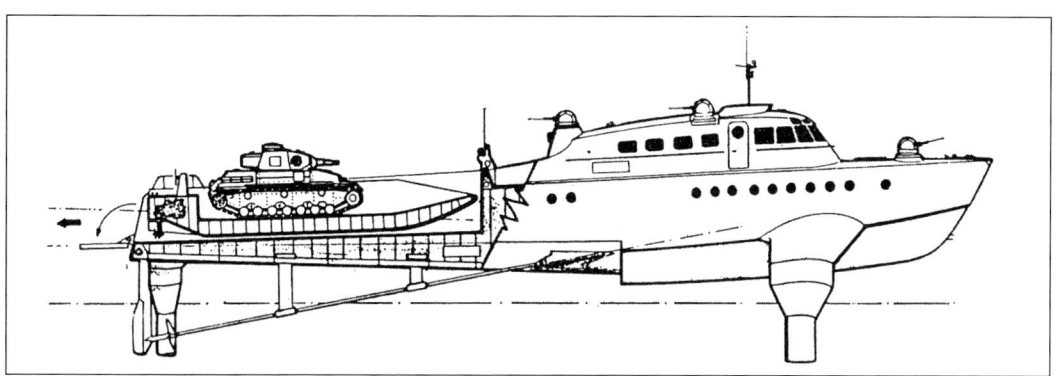

The *VS-8* transport hydrofoil.

Four Luftwaffe 15-mm machine guns were housed in Perspex turrets and the entire complement numbered twenty-two men.

Nonetheless, despite its promising performance, *VS-8* was plagued by corrosion problems even with the use of seawater-resistant alloys. In September 1944, when its strategic importance had already waned, the prototype was abandoned and lost as a result of a series of adverse events during a storm off Hela in the Baltic Sea.

There were several imaginative hydrofoil design projects that never came to fruition. According to information that Harrauer wrote in 2004, perhaps Schertel-Sachsenberg's most unusual concept was a project under development at the Rosslau shipyard that sought to combine the technology of a fast torpedo hydrofoil attack boat with the ability to fully submerge. Today one can only speculate about this potentially risky idea, information predominantly deriving from a few partial drawings recovered with difficulty by the German historian Harald Fock; the original blueprints are now lost.

It is assumed that this submersible would have been approximately 23.5 metres long, with a beam of 6 metres and displacement of 105 tons. The hull, in light alloy, was of a monohedral prismatic shape aft that allowed effective planing at speed on the surface; it could be flooded completely by the opening of traditional style air vents for the diving phase and used compressed air to blow ballast tanks to surface. The control room, the two engine rooms, the electric motor and the battery containers were all interconnected watertight metal

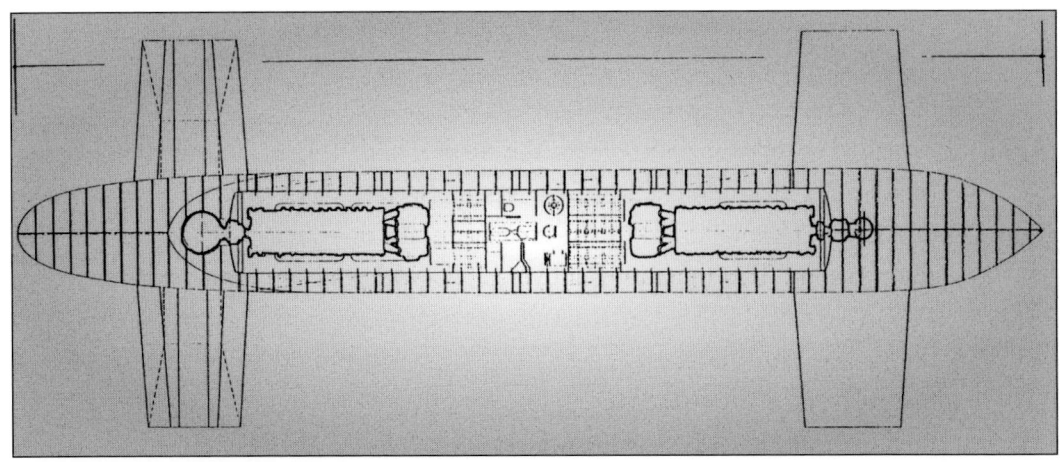

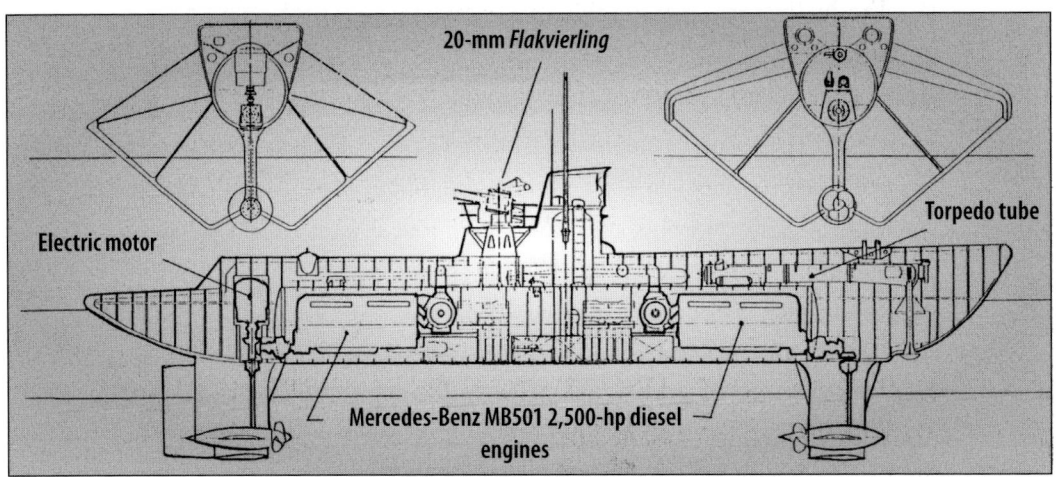

Concept drawings of the Schertel-Sachsenberg 120-ton submersible hydrofoil.

cylinders, constructed in prefabricated pieces and assembled in the shipyard. Harrauer believed that some of these cylinder components were pressure-tested in 1944 and achieved a rated submersion depth of 50 metres. Diving and surfacing were controlled by means of trim and compensation boxes that could be blown with compressed air and it is probable that the hydrodynamic support wings were equipped with moving surfaces allowing them to function as both directional rudders and hydroplanes.

The engines for surface travel would have been two turbocharged Mercedes-Benz MB 501 diesels, each of 2,500 hp, in separate engine rooms, powering two shafts with counter-rotating propellers, installed in the lower structural supports of the rear hydrofoil. The engine room alone occupied 60 per cent of the hull interior space. The expected speed was 45 knots on the surface and 10 knots maximum underwater at snorkel depth, running on diesels. Silent navigation at depth was 5 knots, thanks to an electric motor driving a propeller on the transom. This most unusual vessel would have been armed with two standard 533-mm torpedo tubes, which could only be loaded on the surface. Anti-aircraft defence came via a 20-mm Mauser *Vierling* four-barrel flak installation, mounted to the rear of a small bridge in the configuration customary on U-boats.

Tactically, this craft would have been able to stalk its target while remaining hidden at periscope depth, with the hull either trimmed at depth or resting on the bottom and the crew able to breathe thanks to the snorkel; a methodology relatively easily implemented in the shallower areas of the Baltic Sea, the North Sea or English Channel. The sighting of the enemy would be followed by a rapid surfacing and lightning attack, with an equally fast retreat. However, no example was ever constructed.

Some drawings found in recent times have led to the hypothesis of the existence of additional projects for two small units, dating back to 1942 and 1944, both also capable of operating on the surface with a hydrofoil or submerged in the manner of the above hybrid vessel. The 1942 project involved a hydrodynamic 12-metre single-seater submarine, displacing 4.5 tons, propelled on the surface to a potential speed of 40 knots by a 400-hp diesel engine and underwater at 10 knots with a 200-kW electric motor. The armament consisted of a single underslung conventional 533-mm torpedo. The vessel designed in 1944 would have been an 18.3-metre single-seater coastal torpedo hydrofoil, capable of being disassembled into two pieces – its propeller shaft and hydrofoils removed – and the hull equipped with wheels for transport by tractor. This vessel's attack capabilities amounted to three stern 450-mm torpedoes, with, according to Harrauer, a defensive 13-mm machine gun. Its planned powerplant would have been a 1,500-hp Isotta-Fraschini ASM 184 diesel engine providing a planned 50-knot surface speed. None were ever built.

In fact, Schertel sketched several other designs along these lines, some made into scale models or wooden prototypes demonstrating their technology, but their description would turn into a full-bodied treatise on the study of German fast light units in the decade 1935–45, going beyond the scope of this book.

The Engelmann 'Semi-Submersible' S-boat

Confusingly, there was yet another *VS-5* vessel constructed, now sometimes simply called the 'Engelmann Boat'. This same designation of *Versuchs Schnellboote* was attributed to a semi-submersible torpedo boat designed in 1937 and patented in 1938 by Dr Rudolf Engelmann, described as both an engineer and a dentist.

Engelmann had already begun to research the application of spindle-shaped hull designs that could benefit seagoing ships by enabling greater speed for the same expenditure of propulsive power, his first patent being granted in March 1934. Engelmann's initial designs resemble modern submarines: a fusiform 'cigar-shaped' hull with propeller at the end and hydrodynamic superstructure roughly amidships. His idea was for this vessel to be capable of sailing with the hull submerged and only the superstructure above the water, with benefits in terms of both hydrodynamic and aerodynamic drag as well as increasing the stability of the vessel in rough seas.

Englemann continued to refine his experimental design and update the patent accordingly, until he caught the attention of Korvettenkapitän Max Valentiner, an experienced First World war U-boat commander who went on to work within the Kriegsmarine after its official unveiling to the world in 1935. Once again a civilian technological achievement had obvious military application and Valentiner brought Engelmann's design to the attention of the Naval Construction Office. In December 1937, the powers that were opined that the design possessed a limited application for coastal duties, but could potentially possess greater seaworthiness than existing *Schnellboote*.

The Engelmann *VS-5* semi-submersible torpedo boat moving ahead slowly during tests in Danzig harbour on 10 April 1941. Design speed was 50 knots.

Following appraisal of miniature test models, Engelmann was asked in 1939 to construct a full-sized prototype and a test boat was placed under contract with Deschimag, although the outbreak of war resulted in all construction grinding to an unexpected halt in September and commencement of building postponed. However, Kapitänleutnant Werner 'Fips' Fürbringer, another First World U-boat commander brought out of retirement and becoming an instrumental part of the rebuilding of Germany's U-boat service, had become an enthusiastic proponent of the Engelmann design. He believed that a 600-ton version of the boat could rival an equivalent U-boat in range and speed for coastal operations around Great Britain. If possible it could be equipped with torpedo armament similar to a U-boat of that size and possiblly even two 105 mm deck guns. With a low silhouette above water, the boat could be ideal for night convoy attacks.

Fürbringer had clearly overstated the capabilities expected of Engelmann's vessel, but in 1940 Deschimag received a fresh contract for construction of a 250-ton unarmed test boat. This prototype was a semi-submersible, fast coastal attack torpedo boat, designated *VS-5*. Powered by four MAN L11Z 19/30 11-cylinder diesel engines

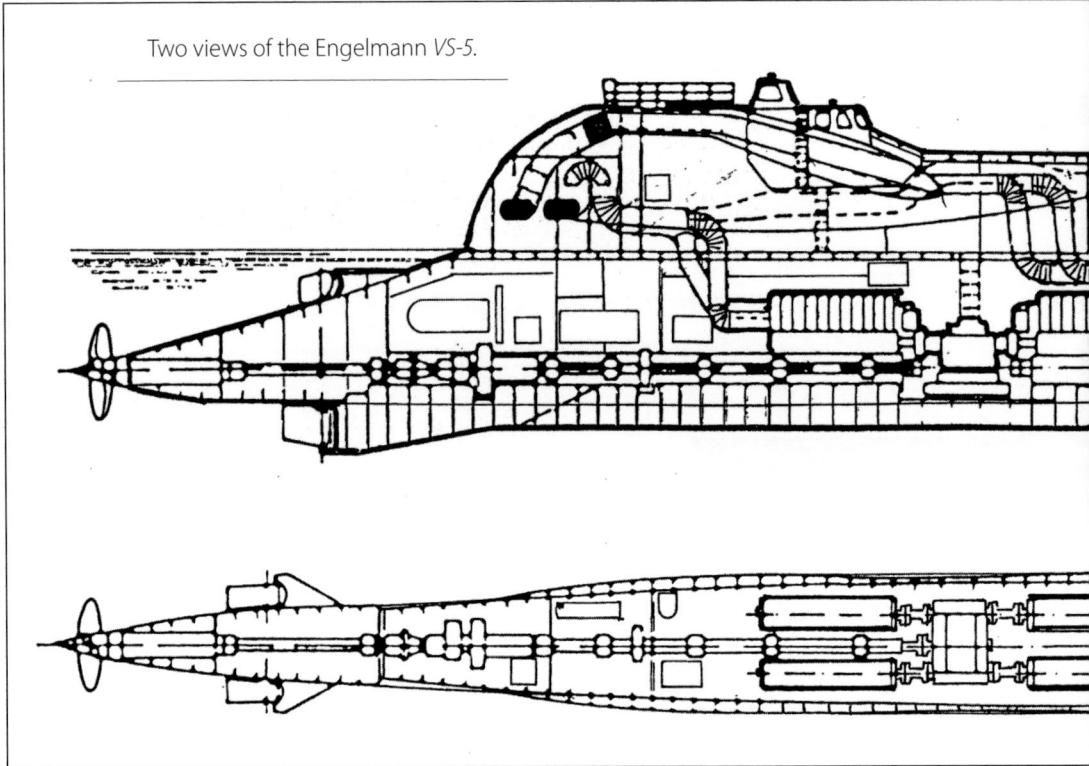

Two views of the Engelmann *VS-5*.

of 1,400-hp continuous output each, installed in two rows within the hull. Measuring 48.84 metres in length and with a beam of 2.82 metres, the keel draught reached 3.6 metres below the waterline. *VS-5* displaced 292 tons and was expected to reach a maximum speed of 50 knots. The craft was theoretically able to submerge fully, although a lack of electric motors or ventilation equipment for operating the diesels meant that it could not move once below the surface.

The boat was launched at Deschimag in Bremen on 14 January 1941 and testing began almost immediately after transfer to the Baltic Sea. Unfortunately, the tests were unsuccessful. At a speed of only 28 knots the ship, due to the torque of the single propeller, began to list up to 14 degrees and above that speed the vertical rudder began to act as a hydroplane; at 35 knots the vessel became virtually unmanageable. This problem could probably have been corrected with either two counter-rotating coaxial propellers, or the adoption of a centreboard and modifying the rudder design but there were

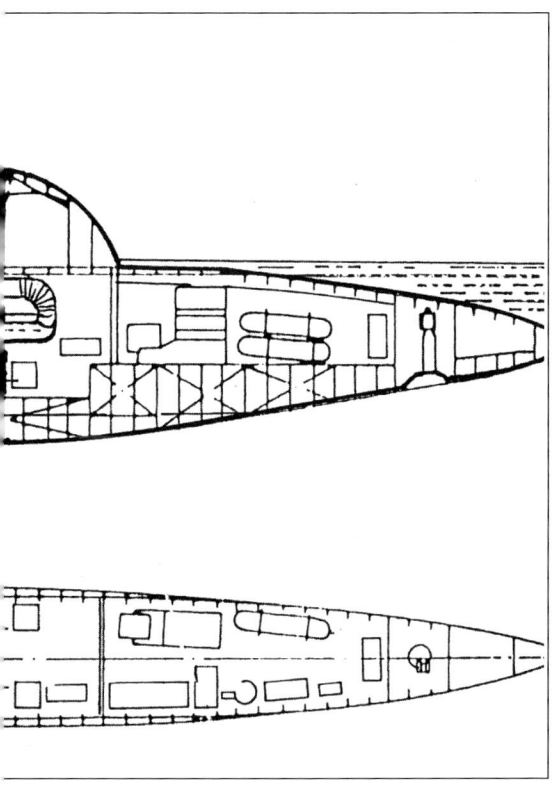

other constructional priorities for the Kriegsmarine and the *VS-5* torpedo boat was soon considered a poor result for the expenditure in man-hours and money that would be required to perfect it. The armament was never installed but was to have included two 533-mm torpedo tubes and two (or more likely four) 20-mm guns. With the Walter U-boat in development at that same time, Engelmann's idea became redundant and the *VS-5* project was abandoned in 1942.

Also related to the Number 5, there are references to several versions of a project known as Wendel *Tragflügelboot* Type 5 or Tr-5. Other elements of the Kriegsmarine – specifically the *Kleinkampfverbände* (Small Battle Units), which included midget submarines, piloted torpedoes, explosive motorboats and frogmen – invested time in planing hydrofoil designs though ultimately to no effect. Tests had been carried out in the Baltic using a small one-man catamaran equipped with a V-1 rocket propulsion system and intended to be armed with a 350-kg explosive warhead in each hull primed with contact detonators. The craft, aptly named *Tornado*, received sea-tests near Peenemünde but displayed problems with this manner of propulsion which gave serious control difficulties at high speeds; it was only capable of operating in calm seas. A final construction version was only completed in May 1945 and was destroyed when Germany surrendered (*see also* pp. 169–70, below).

Nevertheless, the *Kleinkampfverbände* had become interested in developing a small hydrofoil attack boat from these experiments and shipbuilding engineer Friedrich Hermann Wendel created his own designs resulting in the *Typboot-5* and *Typboot-5B* plans, extremely similar to Schertel-Sachsenberg's submersible hydrofoil. Both measured 15 metres in length with a beam of 3 metres and were heavily armed with two F5b 450-mm deck torpedo tubes, ten depth charges, turreted 20-mm *Vierling*, a single gun mounted in the cockpit, and five 86-mm rocket launchers. Despite Tornado's poor handling performance, two Junkers Jumo 004 or Heinkel HeS 011 turbojets and a third central hydroplane were added to *VS-5B* to increase its final top speed to an estimated 65 knots, enabling the fastest possible escape. This vessel is frequently given the name *Seedrache* (sea dragon, a fish similar to the seahorse) but it is possible that this name is an invention of the scale-modelling industry. There is also talk of a hypothetical Tr-5C completely submersible hydrofoil S-boat, on which it is not possible to find any further concrete information. No prototype was ever constructed, and the project remained in the futuristic drawing stage.

However, an idea of how the hull of the Tr-5 might have developed can be had thanks to a post-war realisation patented by the same designer, Friedrich Hermann Wendel, in Germany in 1954 (and the United States in 1959 #2,906,228). A single model built at the beginning of the 1950s, with slightly reduced dimensions and without military equipment, is today visible at the Deutsches Schifffahrtmuseum in Bremerhaven.

Type XI Submarines and LS Torpedo Boats

The history of naval *Wunderwaffen* would not be complete without taking into consideration the various experiments to combine the two new naval warfare philosophies of post-Washington Naval Treaty weapons development with further technological innovations. The Washington Treaty of 1922 had been signed by delegations of the major Allied powers of the First World War and was intended to prevent a naval arms race by limiting construction. Clearly, Germany was not included in this agreement as its potential naval power had already been severely limited by the term of the Versailles Treaty following the end of hostilities. After Hitler's announcement of rearmament and declaration of a new navy – the Kriegsmarine – to replace the Reichsmarine, an Anglo-German Naval Agreement was hurriedly signed to apply similar restrictions on ship size and gun calibre on Germany to those that had already been established in Washington.

Deprived by international agreements of the possibility of building ever larger and more powerful ships, the Kriegsmarine advanced along two paths that over time made it arguably one of the most innovative naval forces of the Second World War: combat by the use of fast vessels, suitable for piracy actions against convoys, and underwater units capable of striking unseen.

An early project taken into consideration during 1937, as part of the search for new naval weapons, was the Type XI U-boat. This was a result of attempts to design a U-cruiser that could operate offensively in distant waters, virtually occupying the role of an auxiliary cruiser, though with the evasion capability of submerging. This U-cruiser would be armed with four 127-mm guns in watertight twin turrets both forward and abaft the conning tower and be capable of operating autonomously at a range of 25,000 km from any home base.

The Type XI was also provided storage for an unarmed Arado Ar 231 reconnaissance aircraft, housed with its wings folded in a vertical pressure-resistant tube 2.25 metres wide and 7.5 metres long, immediately forward of the conning tower. The use of a vertical storage space negated necessity of any further construction on deck with its associated hydrodynamic drag and stability issues. A folding crane on the U-boat's starboard side would be used to remove and later recover the aircraft, which was assembled on deck prior to flight.

Alternatively, a U-boat variant had already been considered with a large, watertight cylindrical hangar of a size sufficient to hold two torpedo boats. Tentatively designated the Type III, the two small torpedo boats could be transported to the vicinity of bays or anchorages where enemy ships were stationed, or even on the high seas in case of encounter with fast merchant ships, whereupon they could be launched to mount a rapid assault. The volume of positive bouyancy deriving from the hangar space would have been compensated during submersion by the weight of the load carried. This included, in addition to the small torpedo boats' 22 tons, the remaining armament which could include forty-eight ground mines and eight torpedoes.

The difficulties that led the Kriegsmarine to abandon the idea of a U-boat carrying torpedo boats or capable of launching aircraft lay primarily in the recovery of the vehicles after deployment, which proved impossible to carry out in rough seas. Eventually, at the tail end of the war, some long-range Type IXD-2 cruiser U-boats would be equipped with a variant of the aerial scout when they carried a Bachstelze unpowered glider, which was launched after assembly on deck and remained tethered to the U-boat but dramatically increased the visible horizon from its high viewpoint. They were used rarely, primarily in the Indian Ocean, where Allied military interception possibilities were sparse.

With abandonment of the projected Type III, the small LS torpedo boats (*Leichte Schnellboote*) were instead intended for use with auxiliary cruisers, the name given to merchant ships converted to military use, frequently referred to by the Allies as 'Raiders'. Considered much easier to launch and recover using heavy cranes aboard these vessels, three of them were embarked on the *Komet*, *Kormoran* and *Michel* and the remainder located in the Aegean Sea following the capture of Greece in 1941, where they had arrived after a transfer by rail.

These boats – thirty-four were intended to be constructed beginning in 1938, though only twelve were completed –

A Type I U-Boat from the 1930s. These became the basis of the planned Type III with a watertight cylinder aft of the conning tower that was to house two LS boats.

were crewed by seven to nine men, 12.5 metres long with a 3.46-metre beam and displacement of only about 10 tons. The prototype was built by the Naglo shipyard, with a mixed structure in light alloy and lamellar mahogany planking.

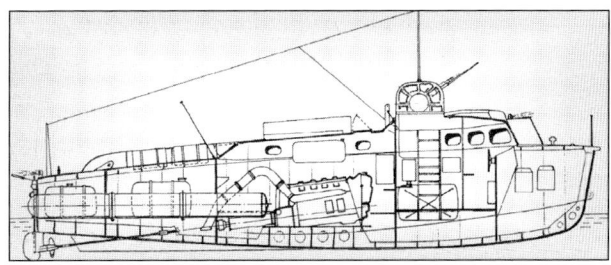

Section of the *Leichte Schnellboot* (LS).

Eleven later units were built entirely in alloy by Dornier Werft in Friedrichshafen. Capable of 38 knots, they were initially powered by two Junkers six-cylinder Jumo 205 aircraft engines, but this powerplant proved ineffective and an enhanced model was upgraded to be powered by reliable Daimler-Benz MB 507 diesels. The main armament included two rearward-facing 450-mm torpedoes or chutes enabling the carrying of up to four mines, and a hydraulically operated Luftwaffe HD151 turret with transparent Perspex that housed a single 20-mm Mauser MG 151 cannon. The torpedoes were launched by a pneumatic system that projected them in the direction opposite to the motion of the boat. Mines were deployed by equipped vessels via a rearward facing chute, while three depth charges could also be delivered by a sloping rearward chute as well as two on each side via racks. On 22 April 1942, in Atlantic waters, *LS-4*, embarked on the *Michel*, sank the 8,684-grt American tanker SS *Connecticut* with two torpedoes, after a long pursuit. Twenty-four of *Connecticut*'s crew were lost as well as eleven Naval Armed Guards. The remaining eighteen survivors were rescued by *Michel* and eventually turned over to the Japanese as prisoners of war. On 6 June *LS-4*, again with the support of *Michel*, torpedoed the 7,176-grt Liberty Ship SS *George Clymer*, 600 miles south-west of Ascension Island. One crewman was killed, before the ship was abandoned, disabled with a broken propeller shaft, and left drifting. Though they reboarded the following day, the crew were finally removed by the British armed merchant cruiser HMS *Alcantara*; attempts to scuttle

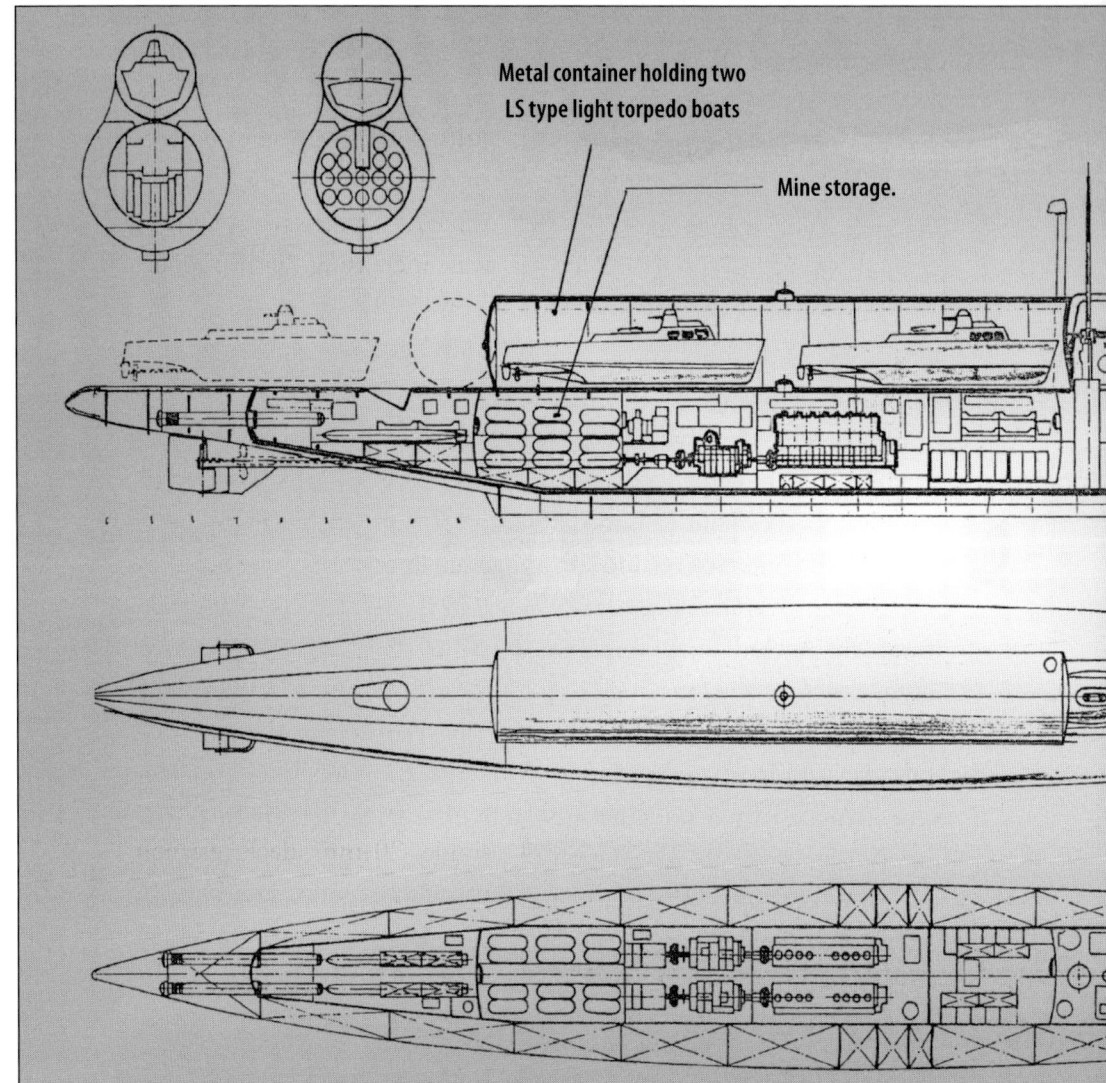

Submarine light torpedo boat carrier; the planned Type III U-boat

the ship outright failed and it was left to sink gradually, drifting and derelict.

The subsequent decline of Germany's auxiliary cruisers' fortunes was not the end of the *Leichte Schnellboote* story. By October 1943 conventional S-boats were spread thinly across the Mediterranean Sea and achieving little. *Marinekommando Italien* requested the allocation

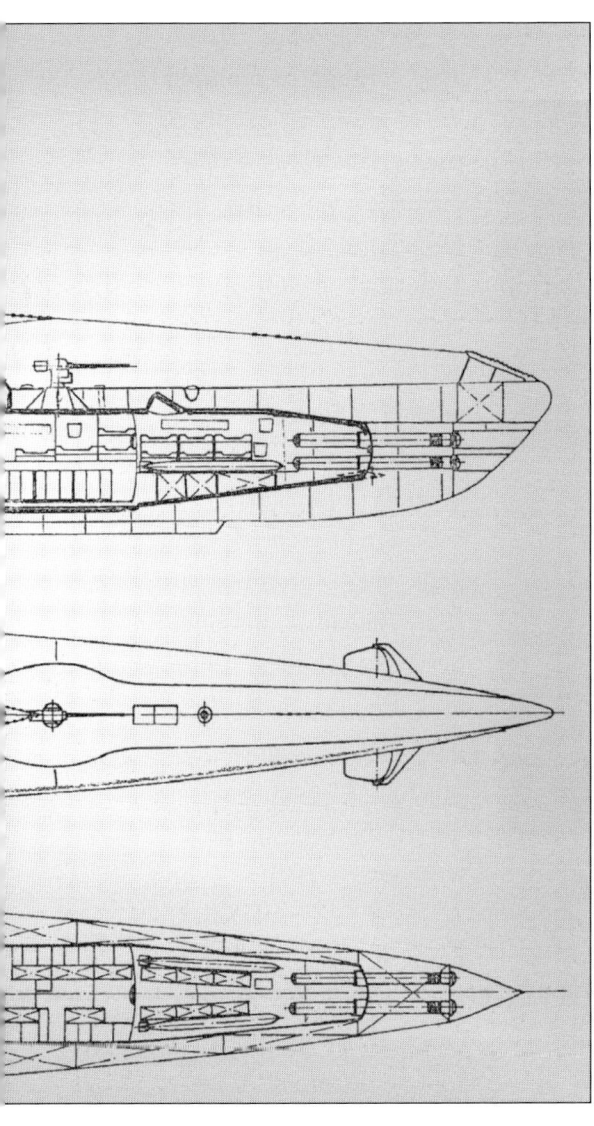

of two further S-flotillas (and one of midget submarines) as a minimum in order to fulfil offensive requirements in the Adriatic where Yugoslavian partisan activity was increasing with support from Allied forces. During October a new sub-command – Kommandierender Admiral Adriatic – was created under the leadership of Vizeadmiral Joachim Lietzmann and the decision was taken to move all S-boats from the western Mediterranean into the Adriatic and Aegean Seas. Already in the Aegean were *LS-5* and *LS-6*, fitted with depth charges and a single 20-mm deck weapon in an enclosed turret. On 15 October, *LS-5* was strafed by seven Allied aircraft northwest of Kos and beached, then later attacked by British MTBs and destroyed.

By the middle of April 1944 a newly established 21st S-flotilla was an ambitious attempt at using the light S-boats that had been originally designed for merchant raiders in the Aegean. Small enough for rail transport from Germany, the first four arrived at the beginning of May. The flotilla was commanded by experienced skipper Kapitänleutnant Ludwig Graser and each boat was captained by a senior petty officer. The last boats arrived in Athens at the end of July.

Two views of an LS-2 'Meteorit' light torpedo boat aboard the auxiliary cruiser *Komet* (the former merchant ship *Ems* adapted to the role of merchant raider). The three ducts that open on the transom were used for laying of magnetic TBM/S mines, since this boat, despite its classification, did not carry torpedoes.

By October 1944, as Germany's fortunes terminally declined, the writing was already on the wall for the LS boats of the 21st S-flotilla. Originally earmarked for offensive action against Allied convoys in the Otranto Strait between the heel of Italy and Albania, a shortage of escort vessels kept them confined to the Aegean, stationed between Rhodes, Leros and Phalerum while a base was planned for Corfu. However, frequent damage in heavy weather resulted in *LS-8*, *LS-9* and *LS-11* being in an Athens shipyard when the general evacuation of German forces from Greece began. The advance of Russian forces in south-eastern Europe threatened to isolate Greece and Hitler had granted Generaloberst Alexander Löhr, commander of Army Group F, permission to withdraw.

During August 1944 Bulgaria had withdrawn from the Axis and declared its neutrality, further weakening the eastern flank. The evacuation of the Aegean islands started at the beginning of September, though the last would not surrender until May 1945. Rhodes was evacuated on 12 September, Allied troops advancing into the power vacuum. Nine days later Löhr began the evacuation of the Peloponnese, western Greece following soon afterward. The LS boats in Athens were destroyed with explosives, while Obersteuermann Breitschuh's *LS-10* was sunk by aircraft on 12 October while escorting a convoy to Salonica that lost thirteen other ships to carrier-borne aircraft from the newly deployed and powerful British Aegean Force.

Remaining 21st S-flotilla personnel joined the march north out of Greece, taking part in land battles alongside elements of XXII Gebirgskorps. Skilled S-boat men were ordered to return to Germany immediately and seventy-four were flown home by Ju 52 aircraft, the remaining 200 fighting against advancing Allied forces and partisans. The last seaworthy boat, *LS-7*, sailed alone into the north Adriatic, running aground near Grado while skirting a minefield. Obersteurmann Erwin Schipke took his six men ashore and they fought their way inland to the Axis base at Palmanova, the stranded boat being destroyed by Allied aircraft. On 15 December, the 21st S-flotilla was officially disbanded.

Cruiser Submarine Seaplane Carriers

During the First World War, the German Imperial Navy had adopted an operational doctrine for its underwater fleet that established its primary purpose as the fight against enemy merchant traffic. For U-boats engaged in long cruises at great distances from the bases, the sighting of approaching ships was a fundamental requirement. However, since at the time the only means of locating the enemy was purely optical, U-boats were handicapped by the low height of their superstructure which did not allow an observation point high enough to provide an adequate horizon.

The only conceivable remedy for this state of affairs was an aircraft, in this specific case a seaplane for reconnaissance. The first idea of using a U-boat to transport a seaplane dated back to a few months after the start of the hostilities and was jointly developed by two officers of the Imperial Navy, Oberleutnant zur See Walter Forsemann and Friedrich von Arnauld de la Perière. While

Forsemann was commander of the early model petrol-powered *U-12* and would later go on to win the coveted Pour le Mérite in 1916 while captaining *U-39*, de la Perière – brother of the soon-to-be famous U-boat commander Lothar – had been placed in command of the first German naval air unit deployed on foreign soil after he established Seeflugstation Zeebrugge on the harbour mole.

On 15 January 1915 an FF29 – a single-engine biplane with floats built at Flugzeugbau Friedrichshafen – became the first plane to be launched from a submarine when it lifted off from *U-12*. The unarmed scout plane was initially lashed to the U-boat forward deck and was to be piloted by de la Perière. The U-boat partially submerged after releasing the aircraft's ties and de la Perière successfully took flight. However, Imperial Navy observers were largely unimpressed, and decided not to use U-boats as aircraft carriers thereafter, though *U-12* completed no fewer than twenty-six missions, transporting a seaplane on the bow deck. Oblt.z.S. Friedrich von Arnauld de la Perière was captured in December 1915 after his FF33 aircraft came down near Nieuport with engine trouble, and a French ship took him prisoner and landed him at Dunkirk. *U-12*, under command of Kptlt. Hans Kratzsch, was rammed and sunk with its entire crew on 10 March 1915.

In the case of *U-12*, however, the use of the aircraft was far from the originally intended role as a reconnaissance aircraft in search of enemy shipping and the very essence of the carrier vessel was distorted. The aircraft was instead used to carry out bombing missions against targets in France and Great Britain. However, since no type of watertight hangar was provided, when the aircraft was on board the U-boat could only navigate on the surface and was not functioning as an attack submarine but rather the aircraft mothership. The results achieved had proved negligible.

Of greater success was the seaplane carried aboard the commerce raider SMS *Wolf* that left Kiel on 30 November 1916 on a fifteen-month voyage, during which it traversed three oceans. *Wolf* carried a Friedrichshafen FF33E seaplane on board for scouting purposes. Named *Wolfchen*, the seaplane played an important part in *Wolf*'s marauding activities and made over fifty flights in this role. During the voyage *Wolfchen* was operated without bearing any national insignia other than the German war ensign, which was flown from the innermost starboard rear interplane strut as occasion demanded. Crewed by L.z.S. Stein and Oberflugmeister Fabeck, the seaplane contributed to the *Wolf* sinking or capturing twenty-eight Allied vessels and returning home laden with booty from its victims.

Revisiting the idea of an aircraft-equipped U-boat, in 1916, Hansa und Brandenburgische Flugzeugwerke in Briest, near Brandenburg an der Havel (better known as Hansa-Brandenburg or Ha-Bra), was asked by the Imperial German Navy to build a seaplane that could be disassembled and stored in a 6-metre long by 1.9-metre diameter cylinder and be capable of being assembled and set up for flight within ten minutes. The chief designer responsible was Ernst Heinkel, who would become a major figure in Luftwaffe development during the Second World War. Born in Grunbach, Baden-Württemberg, Heinkel had long harboured a fascination for flight as the future of transportation and after constructing his own aircraft in 1911 went on to work with Albatros, playing a major role in the design of the Albatros BII reconnaissance and trainer aircraft. After leaving Albatros he worked as Chief Designer and Technical Director for the Hansa-Brandenburg company, creating land- and seaplanes from 1914 onward.

Heinkel conceived the W 20 biplane, a small single-seater unarmed reconnaissance aircraft of mixed construction with high 'T-tail' and wingspan of only 5.8 metres and a wing surface area of 15.82 m^2, and fuselage 5.93 metres in length. The W 20 was powered by an 80-hp Oberursel U.0 rotary engine configured as a rearward facing 'pusher'. The W 20, which could be assembled in 165 seconds and disassembled in 105 seconds, flew in prototype form for the first time in 1917 and immediately showed weaknesses in the wing struts which caused it be heavily damaged and written off shortly after the beginning of tests carried out on the Havel River. For a second prototype, completed in April 1918, the design was strengthened by increasing the wingspan, adding two additional pairs of uprights and modifying the installation of the two stabilising floats. The engine was also replaced with a 100-hp Le Rhône. However, not even this series of modifications made the seaplane satisfactory and in the third model completed before the end of the war in fulfilment of the originally contracted requirements, the two pairs of external uprights were replaced with single ones of different design, though this was not ready for any operational trials before the end of hostilities in November 1918.

Somewhat ironically, during construction of the second prototype, the Imperial Navy decided that aircraft were not, after all, to be carried aboard U-boats, judging that their fabric and wood construction was not able to withstand the rigours of U-boat service.

Nonetheless, the actual performance of the W 20 seaplane was, for that time, assessed as quite satisfactory. It recorded a maximum speed of 117 km/h and ascended to an altitude of 1,000 metres in less than 15 minutes, considered more than sufficient for observation purposes.

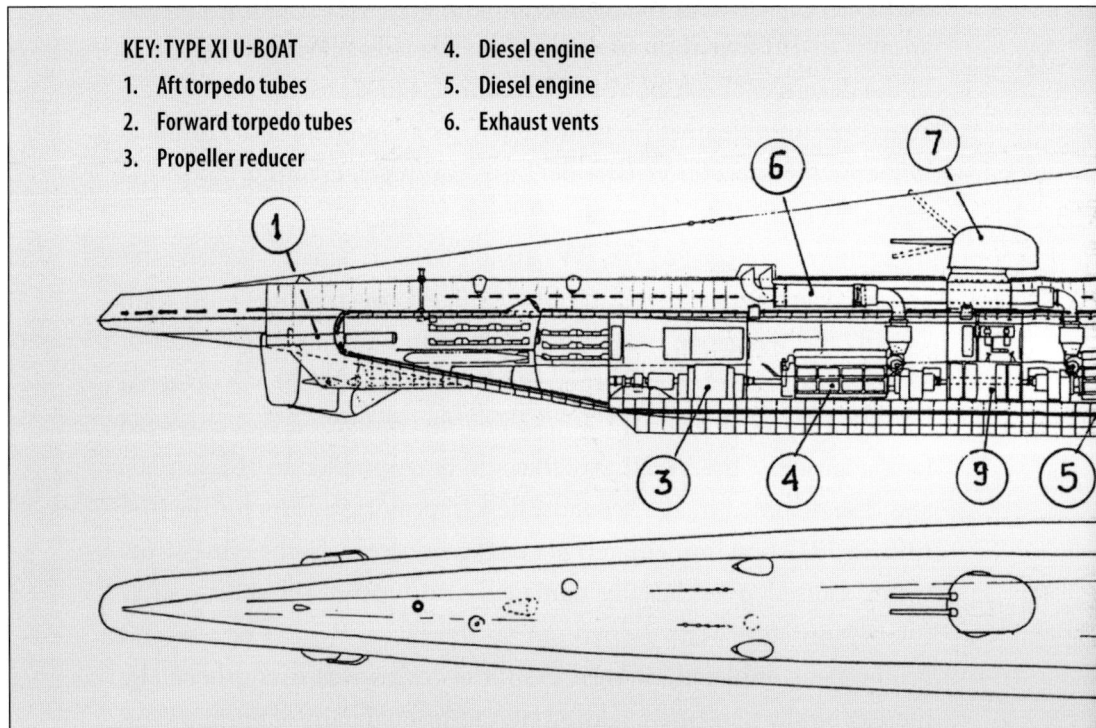

As an alternative to the Heinkel W 20, during the second half of 1918, the Luft-Fahrzeug-Gesellschaft (LFG), using a design by Gotthold Baatz, undertook the construction of a sheet metal-clad, unarmed, low-wing monoplane, designated V 19 (V = *Versuchsflugzeug*, experimental aircraft). This small single-seater aircraft had a wingspan of 9.56 metres, length of 6.60 metres, height of 3.10 metres and a take-off weight of 690 kg. It was powered by a 110-hp Oberursel UR II rotary engine. It, too, was easily disassembled, and the prototype was completed in November 1918 at the Stralsund plant but, due to the armistice and the limitations subsequently imposed by the Treaty of Versailles, its development had to be abandoned. The declared performance included a maximum speed of 180 km/h and a range of 360 km, but not even this second model of seaplane specifically designed with U-boats in mind had any possibility of operational usage.

Following the end of the First World War, by 1921 Heinkel had been appointed head designer of the recently re-established

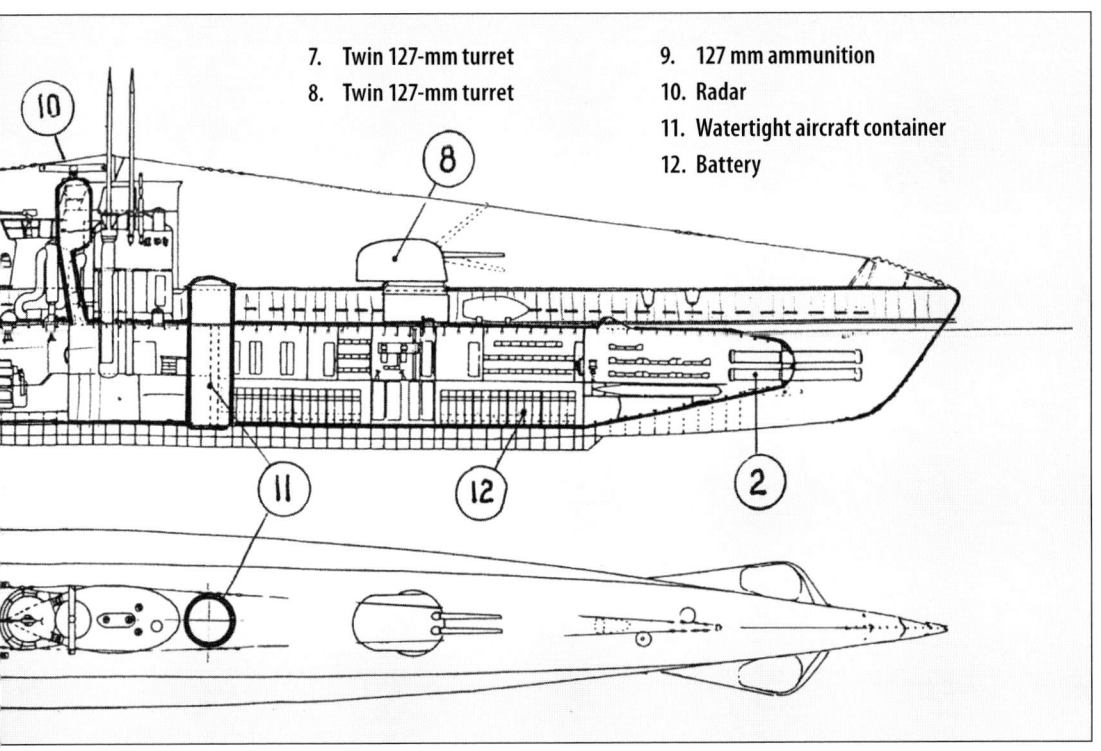

7. Twin 127-mm turret
8. Twin 127-mm turret
9. 127 mm ammunition
10. Radar
11. Watertight aircraft container
12. Battery

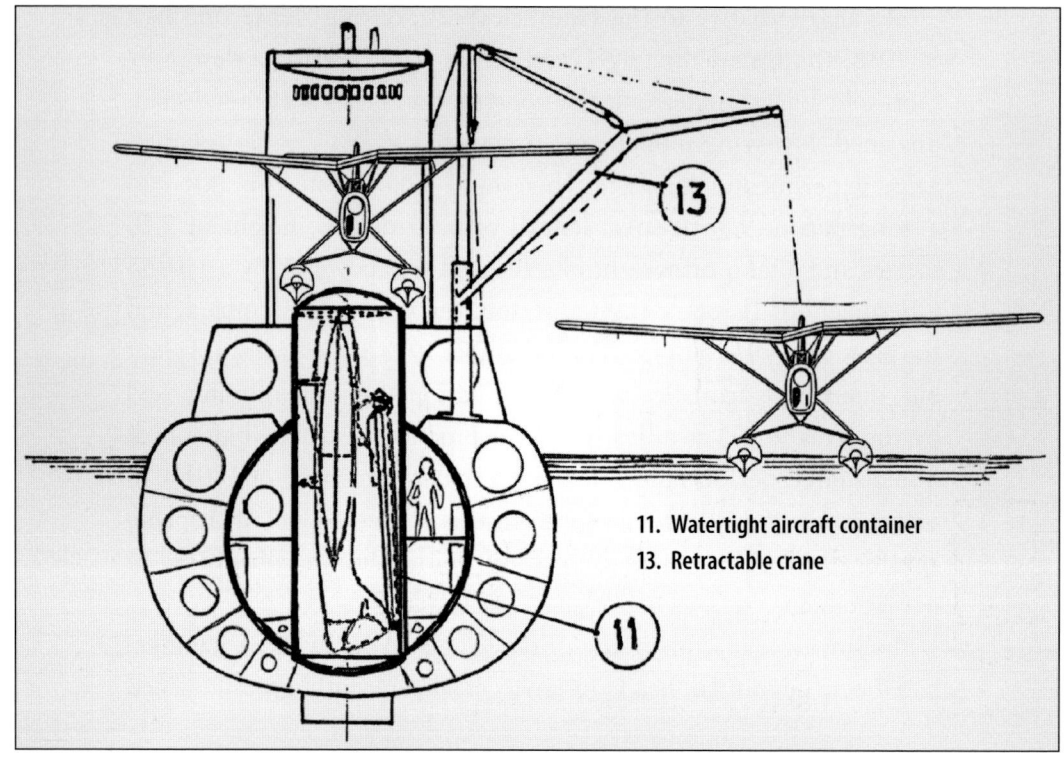

11. Watertight aircraft container
13. Retractable crane

The Arado Ar 231 seaplane reconnaissance aircraft was to be transported, disassembled, inside the vertical watertight container with an upper hatch. With the help of the retractable crane it would be extracted and reassembled on the deck, then put into the sea and could take off and land like any seaplane. Naturally all these operations would have proved precarious with even slightly rough sea and the use of the Ar 231 was abandoned.

Caspar-Werke owned by former naval pilot Karl Caspar. One-time commander of Zeebrugge's naval air station Leutnant Friedrich Christiansen – credited with thirteen aerial victories during the war – approached him to encourage the design of a small floatplane capable of being launched by submarine. In the Pacific, the Japanese–American arms race had begun and both parties were interested in advanced German aeronautical designs. This also provided a welcome means by which to circumvent Versailles restrictions as the actual construction of these licensed designs could take place outside German territory.

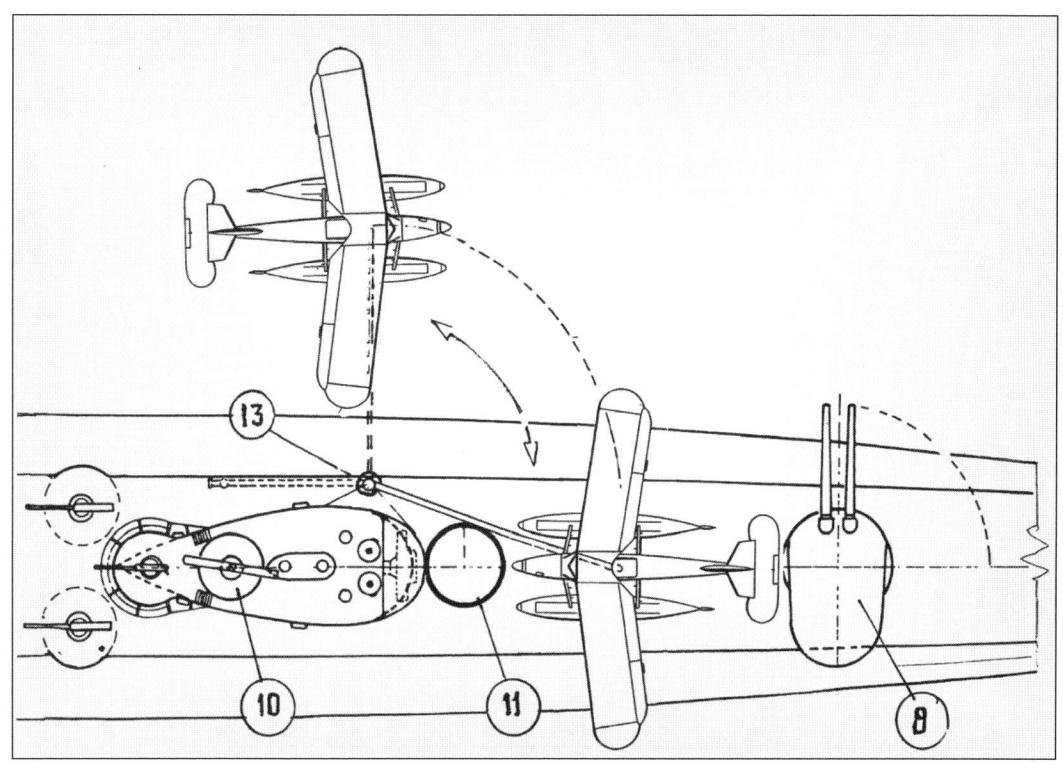

How the seaplane was to be launched from the Type XI after being reassembled.

The Japanese naval attaché in Berlin, Araki Jirō, had already ordered illegal aircraft designs from Heinkel during 1921 (the HD25 and HD26 biplanes) while Christiansen successfully negotiated the construction of a seaplane named 'Caspar U1' for the US Navy. This unarmed cantilever biplane was built entirely of wood and propelled by a 50-hp five-cylinder Siemens Sh 4 radial engine powering a two-bladed propeller. The pilot was housed in an open cockpit behind the upper wing, providing a clear view forward and excellent reconnaissance potential. It could be dismantled so that it could be housed in a 7.4-metre long cylinder with a diameter of 1.7 metres. Because the cantilever design removed the need to rig struts and wires on assembly, the manufacturer indicated that, for a team of four mechanics, the minimum disassembly and reassembly times was between 21 and 33 seconds, though clearly this was far too optimistic to be realistic. However, it could be reassembled on deck in just over a minute on the surface whereupon it was launched by catapult. Two U1 prototypes were bought by the US Navy in 1922 for successful trials, in turn prompting the German Navy to purchase a single U1 aircraft for its own tests. This marked the first naval aircraft ordered since the imposition of the Versailles Treaty, which included an outright ban on German military aircraft, and was an important sign that perhaps naval aviation still garnered some interest in the upper echelons of the Reichsmarine. The Imperial Japanese Navy also ordered two, designated U2 because they had marginal changes compared to the first, but received only one, which was assigned the designation Yokoso Type 1 and would later inform development of the Imperial Japanese Navy's own submarine-carried aircraft the Yokosuka E6Y, while the other remained in Germany and was evaluated by the Reichsmarine.

An improved design – the HS1 – was made for construction by the Swedish Navy, though arguments with Caspar over design rights led Heinkel to depart the company and establish his own design bureau, followed by a construction company – Heinkel-Flugzeugwerke – in a rented ex-naval hangar at Warnemünde. Heinkel thereafter concentrated on design work, his prototypes hidden in sand dunes near his construction hangar and out of sight of inspectors, while larger quantity production took place at the Svenska AB Aero Works in Sweden.

During 1924 Heinkel received orders for catapult aircraft, ship-borne fighters and floatplanes from the Imperial Japanese Navy. After Heinkel once again reminded the Japanese authorities of the ban on German aircraft construction, the Japanese assured him that – as erstwhile enemies from the First World War, and now members of the Allied inspection commission – they would warn him of any pending inspections, allowing incriminating material to be secreted away. The Reichsmarine was already negotiating secretly with its Japanese counterparts to exchange technological information, this proving immensely beneficial also to the reconstruction of the German U-boat service.

The Arado Ar 231

While the Imperial Japanese Navy launched its first submarine capable of carrying an aircraft – the *I-5* – in June 1931, the idea of creating a seaplane submarine received fresh impetus in Germany during the second half of the 1930s when the Kriegsmarine, as part of the massive rearmament programme involving all the components of the Wehrmacht, began planning a U-boat fleet destined to operate mainly in the Atlantic Ocean. The task of meeting the required specification was directly assigned to Arado Flugzeugwerke of Warnemünde, which, with the construction of the Ar 95 and Ar 196, had quickly established a good reputation in the field of floatplanes. Preliminary studies were begun in 1938 by the technical office in Brandenburg, taking into consideration different configurations with the designation E 300 ('E' = *Entwurf* or 'project'). The specifications formulated jointly by the Oberkommando der Marine and the

The small Arado Ar 231 reconnaissance seaplane was designed to be transported, disassembled, aboard suitably equipped submarines. The parasol-type wing had an unusual asymmetrical design.

The prototype of the Arado Ar 231 in one of the photos used for its technical manual. The wings are folded for storage inside the submarine's watertight container.

Luftwaffeninspektion der Marineflieger on 27 February 1939, required a single-engine, single-seater aircraft primarily intended for use with the projected Type XI twin turret U-cruiser. The plane, with wings and floats folded, was intended to be fixed to a sled that would have facilitated its manoeuvring on the deck and housed in a vertical cylindrical pressure-tight container, 7 metres long and 2.25 metres in diameter. On 6 December a full-size simulated prototype was submitted to the Kriegsmarine's technical department for consideration and on 8 January 1940 the definitive order was given for the construction of four prototypes, designated Ar 231.

The seaplane, of metal construction, was a light parasol-wing monoplane with a 160-hp Hirth HM 501A six-cylinder inverted inline piston engine, providing 160 hp and powering a two-bladed fixed-pitch propeller. A wingspan of 10.18 metres, giving an area of 15.2m², length of 7.81 metres and loaded weight of a little over

1,000 kg met the expected criteria, providing an aircraft that was simple and compact which could be removed from its cylinder and reassembled by two men within six minutes. The wings themselves were specifically designed in an offset pattern with the right wing root attached at a point tilting upwards, thereby lower than the left wing for ease of folding into storage.

The first model Ar 231 – V1 – flew on 25 July 1940 and was then transferred to the Erprobungsstelle See in Travemünde, where it was joined by the other three prototypes (the total number of units built was six). However, there the small seaplane displayed a series of potential problems, the most serious of which was the impossibility of recovery on board in anything over a force 5 sea.

The V3 and V4 prototypes were embarked on the auxiliary merchant cruiser Schiff 23 *Stier*, which on 21 May 1942 sailed from the mouth of the Gironde for a cruise against Allied merchant shipping. During the voyage the seaplanes revealed themselves completely unsuitable for the role of embarked reconnaissance and only one of the two prototypes, lightened as much as possible and fuelled with only 50 per cent of its fuel capacity, made a 30-minute flight on 23 August 1942, the only operational mission of an Ar 231. Shortly thereafter, on 27 September, after an engagement with the armed Liberty Ship SS *Stephen Hopkins* both the American merchant vessel and *Stier* were left sinking and with them ended any prospect of further employment for the Ar 231.

Missile Submarines

The idea of a submarine capable of launching self-propelled ordnance was studied by the Reich in parallel with tests of similar land-based weapons systems of this type devised in Germany. In the summer of 1942 the Type IXC U-boat *U-511*, was modified to launch six 30-cm Wurfkorper Spreng 42 rockets from the deck, no different from those used by the Nebelwerfer 42 artillery rocket launcher.

U-511 had been commissioned on 8 December 1941 by exmerchant seaman Kapaitänleutnant Friedrich Steinhoff, undergoing the traditional gruelling working up in the Baltic before spending the week from 31 May to 5 June involved in the rocket trials in Peenemünde. Leader of the German rocket programme, Dr Werner von Braun, was given the use of *U-511*, then still attached to the 4th U-Training Flotilla, for his experiment at launching rockets from a submerged U-boat and it was no coincidence that Steinhoff's boat was chosen as he was the brother of Ernst Steinhoff, a senior scientist at the rocket research establishment at Peenemünde and collaborator with Braun.

Code-named 'Project Ursel', six solid-fuel rockets were installed on the deck of *U-511* in wire traps similar to the Army's half-track mounted Nebelwerfer. The rockets were set at a 45-degree angle, an electrical charge providing the impulse for launching. The tests were positive, showing that the rockets worked not only on the surface, but also up to a depth of twelve metres.

However, the 30-cm Wurfkörper 42 projectiles proved to be almost impossible to aim precisely enough due to the absence of an effective targeting and guidance system, being potentially effective only as a blanket shore bombardment. An initial thought of bombarding the American coast with these weapons was also found to be impractical from a seaworthiness point-of-view. Although Steinhoff stated that he could launch the rockets at a shore target with some hope of success, the boat handled very poorly while submerged with rockets mounted on deck. There was not enough room to accommodate the weapons inside the boat, therefore requiring a whole new design to be thought of.

Karl Dönitz would have liked the development of this technology to continue, thinking of its potential use against convoys escorts, but the absence of an effective targeting and guidance system for this type of rocket led to the idea being abandoned despite satisfactory test firings.

The limited success achieved meant that that was not completely the end of attempts to launch the Nebelwerfer rockets from a submerged U-boat. In the Black Sea the 30th U-boat Flotilla had taken possession of a number of rocket batteries shipped from Germany. Flotilla staff had long been looking for extra possibilities

Testing the rocket installation aboard *U-511* in the Baltic.

for the use of the six small Type II U-boats against Soviet ports in the Caucasus. Artillery had been ruled out, as the stability of the coastal U-boats could not be maintained if an 88-mm deck gun was installed, and smaller-calibre weapons were of little effect. Eventually, three U-boats were used for experiments with the rocket batteries while between patrols; *U-9* and *U-24* used rockets attached to the hull below the waterline and *U-19* had them mounted on the foredeck.

The tests were not without problems. Initially ignition proved uncertain while submerged and then when one shot was successfully test fired it hit the U-boat's own extended periscope. Thereupon it was decided the racks could only be attached to the upper deck and ignition carried out from the conning tower using a loose laid cable rather than any rigid installation. Whether under water or on the upper deck, the problem remained that the only method to aim shots was by aligning the whole boat.

During July 1944 *U-9* was moved into the floating dock at Constanta and, under cover of tarpaulins to prevent any casual observation, two rocket crates were installed; each approximately three to four metres in length and fixed at an angle of between 45° and 60° from the horizontal, one to port and one to starboard. The pressure hull was pierced for the ignition cables and provided with pressure-resistant glands, the cables running into the control room where each was connected to the ignition panel.

The projectiles were introduced on slides from the outside into the square lattice boxes, with electric cables connected to the bottom ignition plate. Reloading at sea was therefore impossible. *U-9* sailed from Constanta with three S-boats and went to periscope depth to attempt firing trials. Observing the experiments from an S-boat were the flotilla chief and other experts. After the U-boat was considered at a safe distance a green flare was fired from the S-boat and the first rocket ignited to starboard. The launch was unsuccessful, the rocket breaking through the water surface and flying over the boat to the port side towards the stationary S-boat, which hastily sped away to safety. A second rocket was then released to starboard which vanished without trace, presumably not reaching the surface. The third test firing threw the projectile far outside the intended direction of flight, impacting at quite some distance. From the port side rack, two ignitions were successful but only one rocket broke the surface, reportedly taking off across it 'like a dolphin'. Despite ambitions to resume testing at a later date a bombing raid on Constanta destroyed the stored rockets.

The major resources of the experimental missile centre at Peenemünde were instead devoted to the world's first cruise missiles equipped with a pulse engine – the V-1 (Fieseler Fi 103) – and to ballistic missiles with a liquid propellant rocket engine. The development of the latter technology achieved with the A4 (Aggregat 4) a missile capable of hitting England from launch sites on the continent, the missile being better known as the V-2,

The 30 cm *Wurfkorper Spreng* 42 rocket. *U511* could launch six of these missiles.

or *Vergeltungswaffe* 2 (Vengeance Weapon 2). This highly advanced technology presented the Germans with the possibility of bringing the war to the Allied nations, particularly that which benefited most by its location far from the main battlefields: the United States of America.

If a missile capable of intercontinental flight was at that time out of the question, then the Kriegsmarine's resourcefulness in the creation of new tools seemed to present a perfect starting point for devising a way to bring a mobile launch pad within 300 kilometres of a target on United States' soil. The idea of a direct launch from a U-boat deck was immediately dismissed due to the dimensions of the missile and on 11 December 1944 the Peenemünde experimental centre hosted for the first time a research committee for the design of a floating launch device that could be towed by U-boat. The study group included Generalmajor Josef Rossman, a qualified engineer and the Army's Weapons Office Chief, engineer Walter Riedel, head of the Technical Design Office and chief designer of the A4, and Dr Dikmann of the Vulcan shipyard in Stettin, a technician specialising in the construction of U-boats. This team, assisted by numerous other experts, took the cover name of Elektro Mechanishe Werke Karlshagen.

The first document issued was a design for a semi-submersible floating platform 45 metres long and displacing about 500 tons, with a cylindrical section with one end equipped with cruciform fins and rudders for directional and depth control. The opposite end was equipped with a hatched dome that could be opened in two sections.

One or two of these gigantic 'silos' could be towed in a horizontal position, by a single U-boat, its depth keeping underwater regulated by ballast and trim boxes like those of an ordinary conventional U-boat. Control adjustment commands as well as the power required to operate the rudders, pumps and all the services related to the launch of the missile were transmitted via a coaxial cable that was attached to the steel towing cable.

In the first compartment of the container, immediately beneath the opening dome, was the warhead of the A4 missile, a tunnel running parallel to the missile beinge quipped with a service ladder to enable access to the various missile systems and allow successful fuelling. The other sections housed the insulated refrigerated fuel and fuel tanks (ethyl alcohol and liquid oxygen); the fuel pump compartment, with its own hydrogen peroxide and calcium permanganate tanks, and the electric trim pumps. At the stern were located the ballast tanks and the rudder controls. It should be remembered that, unlike systems in use today and the proliferation of 'storable' propellants, at the time that the A4 was in operation the tanks of liquid rocket fuel had to be fuelled immediately prior to launch.

Once the U-boat and towed missile were at an effective distance for launching, the command was given from the U-boat to flood the ballast compartments and place the container in a vertical position, with the opening end protruding from the water. The launch personnel would then cross to the cylinder and proceed to fuel the missile, calibrate the accelerometers, and verify that the A4 was perfectly vertically aligned or with an azimuth angle suitable for hitting the selected target. The launch command was then transmitted from the U-boat. When the missile took off a conical deflector, of the type normally used by the A4, diverted the flare of the propulsion gases towards two or more side vents which during navigation had remained sealed by a diaphragm hatch, but were opened at the moment power was applied to the A4.

As soon as the missile left the platform, the hinged hatches were sealed once again and the platform returned to a horizontal position automatically, ballast tanks filling with sea water to stabilise it in preparation for the return journey which, for reasons of autonomy and efficiency, could be entrusted to a different towing U-boat if required. Vulcan shipyards delivered the container prototype on 25 March 1945, while initial series production was also begun before tests had been completed. It was tested in the Baltic Sea, in the waters near Peenemünde; the launch container was code-named 'Prufstand XII' (Test Stand XII). The ultimate goal would have been to have sixty platforms, with which the Reich could have bombarded major American cities at an optimum rate of 500 missiles per month.

American intelligence managed to retrieve information regarding this project and the US Navy launched 'Operation Teardrop'; a concerted plan to intercept U-boats in American waters with the use of escort aircraft carriers and destroyers. After initiation of 'Teardrop' six Type IXC U-Boats were sighted and four destroyed in American waters; fears that these were already carrying missile weapons were very real in Washington. The sinking of the Type VIIC *U-1053*, a model virtually obsolete by that stage of the war, that was conducting tests in the North Sea near Bergen, is often erroneously believed to be linked to experiments with missile technologies. In truth the U-boat sank during the course of deep diving trials in Byfjord north-west of Bergen, the U-boat being seen to surface at a steep angle and then sink rapidly by the stern with all forty-five crewmen lost. The wreck has since been located by the Norwegian Navy. Meanwhile, the last U-Boat model put into service – the Type XXI – was equipped with the Sp-Anlage rocket guidance system, capable of locating naval targets from below the surface, but this technology never went beyond testing due to the end of the war in Europe.

Stealth Treatment for Submarines

The German submarine *U-480* was one of about six Type VIIC U-boats that were equipped with what has been termed the first 'stealth' treatment for submarines. The hulls of these U-boats were covered with *Alberich*, 4-mm-thick sheets of a type of synthetic rubber called Oppanol, worked with a particular design and with the interposition of microscopic air pockets which possessed sound absorbing properties. Named after the guardian of the *Rhinegold* treasure in Wagner's '*Der Ring des Nibelungen*', the individual sheets were secured to the outer hull with adhesive, achieving a 15 per cent reduction in sonar echo reflection as well as acting as sound insulation for the internal machinery of the U-boat. It was claimed that *Alberich* had the ability to absorb sound pulses of frequencies between 10 and 18 kHz though the 15 per cent reduction was not reliable at all depths.

U-1105, a Type VIIC/41, modified with the application of the Alberich 'stealth' coating.

While Allied sonars had a range of about 2,000 metres, *Alberich*-coated Type VIICs could only be detected if they were less than 300 metres distant. The *Alberich* coating soaked up and did not 'return' the sonar impulses, making it more difficult for hydrophones and acoustic buoys to listen to the noise of the unit while it was navigating underwater.

The first U-boat to receive *Alberich* for trial purposes had been the

U-1105 (left) was nicknamed the 'Black Panther' due to its black rubber Alberich coating.

Type IIB *U-11*, covered in the sheeting for initial testing with the 5th U-Flotilla during 1940; testing at sea was difficult as the U-boats and searching apparatus were both subject to the vagaries of differing water temperature and salinity. Kapitänleutnant Georg Peters, a veteran of the First World War, skippered the training U-boat during these trials which, despite difficulties in appraising exact results, proved encouraging and in 1941 a larger boat, the recently commissioned Type IXC *U-67* of the 2nd U-Flotilla had the metre-wide panels applied to the conning tower and U-boat sides, but not the wooden decking, while in Wilhelmshaven harbour. Clamped and cemented in place, the *Alberich* panels were then painted the same colour as the boat, so that they were barely distinguishable. During May 1941 *U-67* passed through the Kaiser Wilhelm Kanal to the Baltic where the *Alberich* was put through its paces once again.

Though the panels themselves were promising, problems were encountered with adhesion, and as panels came loose they caused hydrodynamic resistance and created water eddies that generated excess noise and therefore the direct opposite of what was desired. During most of July 1941, *U-67* lay in Kiel harbour. Most of the *Alberich* panels were removed except those on the conning tower and the bow. Further experiments and sound trials were made in the Little Belt but also proved unsatisfactory. All the remaining panels were removed before *U-67* departed Germany bound ultimately for Lorient and operations.

The captured Dutch *UD-4* – ex Dutch submarine *O 26* – used by the Kriegsmarine as a training boat was similarly tested, though the adhesive issue remained a substantial problem that prevented its use in action. Not until the dawn of the '*Schnorchel* war' in 1944 was *Alberich* used on patrol, *U-480* of the 9th U-Flotilla becoming the first U-boat to enter combat clad in the rubber sheeting which this time used an improved adhesive compound. At first the results were encouraging. Oberleutnant zur See Hans-Joachim Förster took *U-480* from Brest in early August bound for the English Channel and shipping bound for Normandy. He sank the corvette HMCS *Alberni*, minesweeper HMS *Loyalty* and badly damaged SS *Fort Yale* north-east of Barfleur before moving on to attack convoy FTM74 on the afternoon of 25 August. The convoy overran the submerged U-boat, the din of propellers easily audible throughout the German hull. The 5,712-ton straggler SS *Orminster* was then torpedoed 35 miles north-west of Cap d'Antifer by Förster after which *U-480* was hunted for seven hours but escaped, his ability to avoid detection apparently enhanced by the *Alberich* covering that had been applied the previous May.

Förster's enthusiastic endorsement of the qualities of *Alberich* supported the decision that had been made in June to equip numerous upcoming Type XXIII and Walther XXVI U-boats with it, though due to the lack of a suitable covered space with which to coat the planned two to three Type XXIIIs per month with *Alberich*, the first – and only – Type XXIII so equipped was not ready for service until February 1945 when *U-4709* was commissioned. It was at one point suggested that the huge unfinished 'Valentin' bunker in Bremen be given over to *Alberich* fitting, though the plan was shelved. In total more Type VIICs ended the war with *Alberich* coatings despite that fact that for every one of this type covered, two and a half smaller Type XXIIIs could be so treated. Only one Type XXIII, *U-4709*, received the panels and, commissioned on 3 March 1945, it never passed out of the 5th U-training Flotilla before the war's end when ObltzS Paul Berkemann scuttled it at the Germainawerft dockyard in Kiel. The only U-boats that undertook at least one war patrol with *Alberich* applied were Type VIICs *U-480*, *U-247*, *U-999*, *U-485*, *U-486* and *U-1105*.

A U-boat snorkel head with *Tarnmatte* synthetic rubber treatment.

For Förster and *U-480* the war ended on 29 January 1945 in the English Channel south-west of Portsmouth, when the U-boat struck a mine in the British field Brazier D2 with all forty-eight hands aboard killed. The wreck was found by divers in 1997.

Material of a similar nature that was more commonly used was *Tarnmatte*, a compound of synthetic rubber and iron oxide powder that coated the head of a U-boat's *schnorchel* that emerged when the U-boat was running on diesels at periscope depth. *Tarnmatte* absorbed enemy radar waves, being claimed to reduce by 90 per cent the return signal given to the British ASV Mk III airborne radar.

PART II

Piloted Torpedoes and Midget Submarines

While the midget submarine can perhaps trace its roots to the origins of the submarine itself – the first designs were in fact small and only suitable for coastal use – the piloted torpedo is often considered 'a weapon of desperation', derived from the need to best exploit the few military resources available to a nation under pressure, even if in the face of greater risks for the human operator. Therefore, perhaps this best represents, more than many other weapon systems, the general state of mind of the Kriegsmarine facing almost certain defeat in the Second World War.

Neger, Marder and *Hai*

By 1943 there was awareness in Germany that the war would probably soon reach ever closer to the homeland of the Reich itself. The Kriegsmarine, with Grossadmiral Karl Dönitz now its commander, firmly concentrated its remaining resources on the war against Allied maritime traffic across the Atlantic, led by its U-boats. On land, coastal defence installations were built and manned by men from all three services, the strongest portion being the vaunted Atlantic Wall which trailed from the north of Norway to the Franco-Spanish border. Further possibilities for coastal defence also became apparent with a concept new to the Kriegsmarine, that of small maritime weapons manned by minimal crew, leading to the establishment of what became known as the *Kleinkampfverbände* (Small Battle Units) under the watchful eye of career naval officer Konteradmiral Hellmuth Heye. These were initially conceived in an attempt to emulate the best offensive exploits of the Italian Decima Mas and Britain's X-Craft and 'Chariot' riders which had proved so effective.

Dönitz originally wanted Heye to become the 'Mountbatten of the German Navy' in reference to Lord Louis Mountbatten, for a time the head of British combined operations. In essence the *Kleinkampfverbände* were therefore intended more as a naval commando force, something that had not yet existed within the Kriegsmarine, though the Army already had the established 'Brandenburger' Regiment, soon to become a more conventional unit with its original methods usurped by specialised SS commandos. Heye's remit was initially to develop and build small torpedo carriers, training naval commandos capable of attacking enemy harbours and installations, develop single-use small submersibles In time it would compose several different branches encompassing frogmen, midget submarines, explosive motorboats and the so-called 'piloted torpedoes'.

The prototype of the *Neger* piloted torpedo conceived in 1943, of which about 200 were built. It was the initial member of the family, in which the piloted torpedo and live 533-mm G7e torpedo were the same length, 7.6 metres.

The first of this last type of weapon, the *Neger* (Negro), came about through a suggestion made by Naval Construction Advisor Richard Mohr, an engineer at the Torpedo Research Department (TVA) in Eckernförde. Mohr had a relatively simple theory that he expounded to his immediate superiors on 21 December 1943. A single electric torpedo would have its warhead removed and rudimentary lateral controls fitted operated by a joystick in a compartment able to house a single operator. Beneath this would be slung an active torpedo which could be piloted to within lethal range of a target and released with a simple lever which would ignite the motor and detach the weapon. The operator could then steer the pilot torpedo back to friendly shores, and scuttle if necessary, although the dome could only be removed from the outside.

A single-shot, relatively inexpensive weapon, large numbers could theoretically be produced which could equip a large unit posing a significant threat to massed shipping such as would be required for an enemy landing on the shores of occupied Europe. Dönitz himself later summed it up when he stated that: 'We require four years to complete a battleship . . . but only four days to prepare ten one-man torpedoes.' It could form part of the ideal naval defence.

On 18 January 1944, as well as approving construction of midget submarines (covered in later pages), Hitler endorsed the construction of the one-man 'piloted torpedo' designed by Mohr and now officially designated *Neger*.

It was a simple if rudimentary device, comprising a standard 533-mm G7e electric torpedo, in the front of which had been created a narrow cockpit surmounted by a Perspex dome which was actually a nose-gunner's bubble from the Dornier aircraft factory in Friedrichshafen. Control of the vehicle was limited to very simple commands: the pilot could decide speed and direction, while for depth he could only rely on slight dynamic submersion using thrust and the tiny incremental adjustment to inclination available; the *Neger* was designed to operate surfaced. The greater lateral movement was provided by external pull rods in place of the standard G7e stern fins. Enclosed beneath the dome, the operator's air supply was sufficient for only seven hours at 4 knots before risk of suffocation, and more equipment borrowed from the Luftwaffe provided the answer with a Dräger-type closed-circuit respirator supplying air through a fighter pilot's face mask. Propulsion was provided by a 12-hp electric motor, which guaranteed a maximum speed of 18 knots, but ideal cruising speed was around 4 knots, at which it could have a range of 48 km.

This, then, was the carrier vehicle. Suspended vertically under the hull there was a second standard G7e, with its 279-kg warhead intact, which constituted the armament. Small, graduated markings along the lower edge of the dome could be aligned with a vertical rod welded to the carrier torpedo nose to provide a rough aiming device. The entire complex weighed in total 2,780 kg.

During initial Baltic trials ObltzS Johann Krieg took the pilot torpedo into the Baltic with only a rubberised canvas 'spray

A Neger piloted torpedo under way.

Neger Technical Details	
Displacement:	2.7 tons
Length:	7.6 metres
Diameter:	0.533 metres
Propulsion:	AEG-AV 76 electric motor, 12 hp (8.8 kW), + 12 × Type 13 T210 batteries
Speed:	3.2– 4.2 knots (5.9–7.8 km/h) on surface
Range:	48 naut. miles @ 4 knots (89 km @ 7.4 km/h) on surface
Crew:	1
Armament:	1 × G7e 533-mm torpedo

skirt' protecting him and the torpedo interior from the elements. With only his goggled head showing, this was soon found utterly impractical, leading to the addition of the Perspex dome. However, this too was not without problems. Visibility was poor due firstly to an unfortunate positioning of the pilot, too low compared to the dome with his eyes at about sea level, and secondly to the ease with which floating oil waste and debris could accumulate against the dome. Furthermore, with the vessel unable to dive, night operational trials soon showed that the Perspex could reflect bright moonlight and potentially expose the vehicle to the enemy. An attempt to convert the *Neger* to a submersible saw a small diving cell fitted to the carrier torpedo, capable of being flooded and allowing the *Neger* to submerge. However, this was soon abandoned as trim proved impossible to control and the test vehicle buried its nose in the seabed. Furthermore, the space required to hold the compressed air tank needed to blow the cell free of water and surface reduced battery storage capacity by too great a margin. The *Neger* would see action as it was.

Though it took some time to realise, the *Neger*'s ideal successor took the name of *Marder* (Marten) and, though outwardly similar, had involved a complete redesign of the forepart of the carrier torpedo. The carrier torpedo was lengthened by 65 cm – increasing the 7.6-metre length of the *Neger* to around 8.25 metres – enabling the *Marder* to incorporate a pressure chamber immediately behind

Marder Technical Details	
Displacement:	3 tons
Length:	8.3 metres
Diameter:	0.533 metres
Propulsion:	AEG-AV 76 electric motor, 12 hp (8.8 kW), + 12 × Type 13 T210 batteries
Speed:	3.2–4.2 knots on the surface (5.9–7.8 km/h)
Test depth:	40 metres
Range:	48 naut. miles @ 4 knots (89 km @ 7.4 km/h) on surface
Crew:	1
Armament:	1 × G7e TIIIb 533-mm torpedo

the pilot's seat which carried 200 kg of compressed air which could be used to blow the 30-litre flooding tank located in the nose. The extension of course increased the displacement of the *Marder* to 3m³ over the 2.7m³ of the *Neger*, but with approximately 10 kg of compressed air used each time the diving cell was blown, the *Marder* could submerge up to twenty times. Furthermore, the torpedo carried was a G7e TIIIb, specially lightened from the normal G7e weight of 1,760 kg to 1,352 kg by the removal of half the batteries, giving a reduced speed and range of 18.5 knots and 4 kilometres. This measure was taken in order not to swamp the carrier vehicle and overwhelm any ability to trim the *Marder* after torpedo discharge and corresponding sudden loss of weight.

Further improvements included a hinge fitted to the Perspex dome making it possible to secure and release it from inside the *Marder*. There was an iron ring fixed inside the manhole and moved by use of a special key that caused it to press securely against a separate ring and squash a watertight rubber gasket between them. A small depth gauge graduated to a maximum of 30 metres was included as was a spirit level on the left hand side of the cockpit that showed the angle of tilt up to ±15°. Further gauges in the cockpit monitored pressure within the pressure chamber, oxygen container and cockpit.

The first batch of forty volunteer *Neger* pilots assembled at Eckernförde and had been drawn from all three branches of the

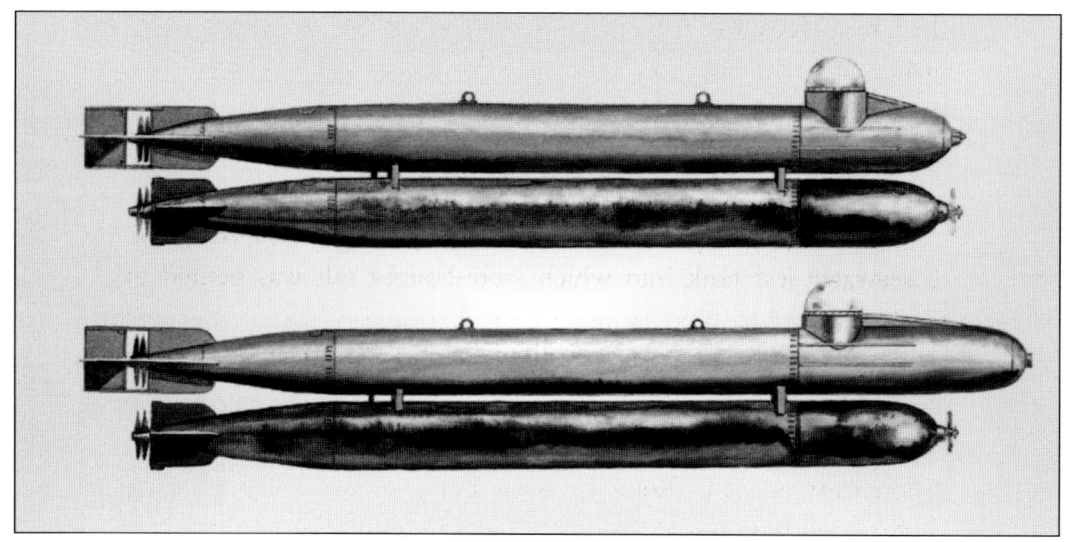

Comparison of the *Neger* (top) and the slightly longer *Marder*.

Wehrmacht as well as the Waffen-SS. There Sonderführer Michael Opladen instructed them in basic torpedo shooting, seamanship and navigation. Training was arduous and at least one man was killed during Baltic exercises when his practice torpedo failed to detach on ignition and, unable to release the cupola from inside, he was killed as the carrier torpedo was dragged along the underside of the target ship's hull. When made operational, they were designated the 361st K-Flotilla.

The best documented action conducted with piloted torpedoes was perhaps their baptism of fire on the night of 20/21 April 1944. Following their successful training, the forty *Neger* pilots and their torpedoes – given the cover designation Marine Einsatz Kommando (MEK) 175 for this operation and under the command of ObltzS Johann Krieg – were transported to Italy to attack Allied naval units in the Tyrrhenian Sea that were operating in support of the Allied Anzio landings which had taken place in January 1944 in an attempt to outflank the formidable 'Gustav Line' and threaten Rome. However, once ashore, the Allies had been slow to move as immediate commanders appeared confused as to their strategic goal. By the time they had amassed a formidable force, the Germans had reinforced the hitherto thin defending line at Anzio and a grinding attritional battle followed. Traditional U-boats had proved ineffective against the landing and its supporting naval and supply contingent, and Krieg's MEK 175 was provided the opportunity to prove its worth.

Before departing Eckernförde, a single *Neger* was placed in a seawater test tank into which store-bought salt was poured to replicate the increased salinity of the Tyrrhenian Sea as compared to the Baltic. Adjustment to the torpedo trim was made by small ballast weights, replicated aboard all other vehicles before they were entrained for Italy. The Germans had planned to bring the piloted torpedoes to Rome by train, but pinpoint Allied bombing interrupted the railway line at Rignano Flaminio. There the *Negers* were disembarked and taken by trailer drawn by Sdkfz 9 heavy artillery half-tracks to Pratica di Mare, only 20 km from Anzio, where they were hidden in the pine forest near the now abandoned airport. Three had slipped from their transports and been damaged beyond repair during transit, leaving thirty-seven operational.

The coastline was scrubby and low sloping, presenting potential launching problems. The 5-ton *Negers* would need to be brought, with difficulty, by trolley to the beach of Tor Vaianica so Krieg commandeered 500 German *Fallschirmjäger* (paratroops) of a nearby training unit attached to the 4th Fallschirmjäger Division for additional manpower. The pneumatic tyres of the carriages were of aeronautical origin and moved with difficulty over the rough ground, some being punctured, and he therefore it found necessary to resort to civilian labour to level the approach area, with the risk of compromising the secrecy of the operation.

Krieg planned to use the darkness of the new moon period – 20/21 April – to mount his attack, this coinciding fortuitously with an Allied convoy reported approaching the Anzio beachhead. The *Fallschirmjäger* were assembled, pilots sealed inside their carrier torpedoes and from the chosen beach, the first machines were pushed down six runways of coconut matting laid to provide firm footing. Each *Neger* would need to be manhandled with difficulty into the sea and far enough along the gently sloping seabed until a depth of 2 metres was reached and the *Neger* could depart.

Problems occurred almost immediately. Though the thick matting initially prevented the heavy burdens bogging down in sand, it ended short of the water's edge and several *Negers* became stuck fast, some toppling over as the men tried to heave them free. The matting itself became waterlogged and began twisting inside the axles of some trolleys and over the following hours a total of 14 *Negers* were abandoned at the launching point and later blown up.

The remaining twenty-three sailed in three groups: Group One, under the command of ObltzS Leopold Koch, an ex-U-boat officer and holder of the Iron Cross First Class, was bound for Nettuno Bay; Group Two – the largest – was commanded by LzS Seibicke and would search the Anzio roadstead for whatever shipping could be found; Group Three, five *Negers* commanded by Oberfähnrich Karl-Heinz Potthast, would hunt within Anzio harbour.

Navigation was difficult, visibility almost zero, a wrist compass the only orientation tool supplied to the pilots and of little help, most relying on their crash course in celestial navigation given at Eckernförde. Many simply got lost, overshooting their objectives or sailing on to the open sea. The flotilla as a whole should have proceeded south until 0200 hrs then turned east. The Germans had devised a fairly noisy signalling system to indicate the extent of their lines ashore: an artillery barrage was to continue, while a 20-mm fired a line of tracers every twenty minutes to indicate the direction of Anzio. This method didn't provide much assistance and the mission ended in failure.

Allied intelligence obtained from intercepted Luftwaffe and Kriegsmarine Enigma messages had forewarned of an attempted attack by 'two-man torpedoes' and a special state of alert was ordered throughout Allied naval forces, codenamed 'Wideawake'. Intense patrolling and the random dropping of depth charges on the periphery of the Allied anchorage took place, and USS *PC 591* reported the first radar contact with a *Neger* north-west of Anzio, though the target was never visually detected. The first definite contact came when Oberfähnrich Walter Schulz was sighted by *PC 558*. His canopy was hammered with 40-mm and 20-mm cannon fire and two depth charges were dropped; the miraculously unharmed Schulz was later rescued and taken prisoner.

Ultimately at least four of the attacking *Negers* were sunk and another ran aground on the beach of Anzio; its pilot a volunteer of only seventeen, was taken prisoner. Eighteen pilots found a way back to their launching point by 1000 hrs the following day, but only eight *Negers* were deemed to be reusable. One Neger was later found upside down after grounding on friendly territory, with the pilot dead from asphyxiation as he had not been able to get out of the dome.

Ten had reached their target areas and they claimed some success. The group at Nettuno found no targets and fired their torpedoes

A Neger washed up on shore near Anzio is inspected by American troops.

landward in the hope of striking something worthwhile. Three of the five bound for Anzio harbour passed sentries on the concrete mole and fired at gathered shipping, reporting explosions amongst a cluster of small vessels. However, there are no Allied records of any damage that can be attributed to MEK 175. To compound problems for the Germans, one *Neger* was recovered by the Allies intact and slowly circling with its pilot dead from asphyxiation. Whatever element of surprise the Germans had hoped for with this novel weapon was gone for ever.

However, 361st K-Flotilla later carried out some other operations crowned with positive results in French waters during June and July, including the sinking of destroyer HMS *Trollope* off Sword Beach, three minesweepers in the Seine estuary – HMS *Cato*, *Magic* and *Pylades* – and the Polish cruiser ORP *Dragon* in the approaches to Caen. Damage was also inflicted on the old battleship *Coubert* on the night of 15/16 August 1944, although the ship had already been sunk as part of an artificial harbour. Losses were extremely heavy among the *Neger* pilots and none of the operations could be deemed particularly successful or of any real effect on the battle for Normandy. One pilot, Oberfernschreibmeister Walter Gerhold, a former clerk, was awarded the Knight's Cross on 6 July for his claimed destruction of an enemy 'cruiser', in fact HMS *Trollope*. He was the first man of the *Kleinkampfverbände* to be given the decoration.

Less successful were *Marder* operations, following the deployment of some naval assault units of the Kriegsmarine and the Fascist Italian Republican National Navy (*Marina Nazionale Repubblicana*) in the Ligurian Sea, to counter the activity of the Allies in the waters off southern France. On 5 September 1944, destroyers had hit German positions near the Principality of Monaco with their artillery and twelve *Marders* of ObltzS Peter Berger's 364th K-Flotilla were launched from the small village of Menton to face them. Their journey from Germany had been arduous and difficult due to the dislocation of railway and road networks caused by bombing. The *Marders* eventually gathered in a disused railway tunnel to be readied for action while the pilots were billeted in a hotel in Ospedalette.

At 0810 hrs lookouts aboard the French destroyer *Le Malin* and USS *Ludlow* standing before Cap Ferrat, the peninsula between Villefranche and Beaulieu, sighted the reflection of sunlight on the Perspex domes of the approaching *Marders*. Problems during the difficult launch meant that only five *Marders* managed to make it to their operational area, from which only one would return in the end.

Le Malin opened fire on the closest piloted torpedo, which dived, while *Ludlow* raced at full speed towards another *Marder*, dropping depth charges. At 0848 hrs a piloted torpedo emerged and its pilot surrendered to the crew of the American ship, followed shortly thereafter by another against which *Ludlow* had aimed its artillery. Three prisoners were taken, all pilots who successfully abandoned their sinking *Marders*; a fourth was possibly killed by depth charges.

Walter Gerhold, Knight's Cross winning *Neger* pilot.

On 10 September, after a bout of bad weather had prevented operations, there was a new attack on the US Navy destroyers that were bombarding German positions around Menton. Fourteen *Marders* of ObltzS Hans-Georg Barop's 365th K-Flotilla and ObltzS Paul Heinsius' 366th K-Flotilla, both newly arrived from Germany, were launched between Menton and Ventimiglia alongside three German and three Italian assault boats. Destroyer USS *Hilary P. Jones* forced a *Marder* to surface and hit it hard, completely destroying it and its pilot. USS *Madison* sighted the dome of an approaching *Marder* at 0718 hrs and began to zigzag to avoid any torpedoes, while opening fire with 40-mm Bofors guns, supporting PT-boats also attacked the incoming *Marders* with 20-mm cannon. At least one was forced to dive, reappearing shortly afterwards to be hit again, following which the pilot surrendered.

A reconnaissance aircraft also intervened and *Madison* cruised in the area for five hours, claiming to have destroyed four *Marders*, while the crews of the PT-boats and aircraft claimed to have disabled another five. One survivor who successfully returned to German lines had been wounded and his Perspex dome shattered by cannon fire. No hits were claimed.

The destroyers were later joined by the old French battleship *Lorraine* to bombard the area between Menton and Ventimiglia where it was believed that the insidious vehicles were quartered and, according to German sources, sixteen *Marders* were destroyed on the ground by air and naval attacks. Surviving Marders were moved first to San Remo and then onwards to Treviso, judged to have been ineffectual against moving targets and destined to be held in reserve.

On the night of 18/19 December fourteen *Marders* attacked Allied warships off San Remo that were harassing German troop

Hai Technical Details (assumed data)

Displacement:	6 tons
Length:	11 metres
Diameter:	0.533 metres
Propulsion:	AEG-AV 76 electric motor, 12 hp (8.8 kW), powered by 12 × Type 13 T210 batteries
Speed:	3.2–4.2 knots on the surface (5.9–7.8 km/h)
Test depth:	40 metres
Range:	48 naut. miles @ 4 knots (89 km @ 7.4 km/h) on surface
Crew:	1
Armament:	1 × G7e TIIIb 533-mm torpedo

One of the few known images of the piloted torpedo *Hai*, the final member of the *Neger* and *Marder* family, which had a new propulsion system.

concentrations. Only six returned, all without experiencing any success; five reported misses either through their own inaccuracy or as a result of torpedo failure. Of those lost, nineteen-year-old Wolfgang Hoffmann was captured along with his intact *Marder* after he grounded during an attempted attack on Menton harbour, being pulled from the *Marder* by American troops before he could set off its scuttling charge.

To improve the characteristics of the *Marder*, a fresh design of the piloted torpedo concept named *Hai* (Shark) was created. The carrier torpedo was much longer to make room for the electric propulsion system of the G7e/T111d 'Dackel' (*Dachshund*) torpedo, a low-speed long distance torpedo measuring 1,100 cm in length with an extended battery compartment, granting *Hai* potentially greater autonomy in action.

Only two illustrations of this piloted torpedo are known, in each of which the length appears distinctly different. The most generally accepted explanation has it that the carrier torpedo (which in the *Neger* was 7.6 metres long and in the *Marder* 8.3m) reached 11.2 metres but that an experimental prototype had also been built that was capable of lateral navigation, but not diving, with a length of around 13 metres due to additional depth rudders at the head of the explosive torpedo. The latter in the standard version had to be the G7e/T5 *Zaunkönig* (Wren) or a similar variant with the *Hase* (Hare) acoustic guidance system. For this reason some sources indicate that this last German achievement in the field of piloted torpedoes was named *Hai/Hase* or simply *Hase*.

The single constructed prototype *Hai* was tested in 1945 with discouraging results and the programme was soon abandoned. In other writings dedicated to German secret weapons there are also references to *Marder II* and *III* variants, but without any clear indication on which aspects would have differentiated them from the basic *Marder* type.

It is important to note that the term 'human torpedo' is commonly used in conjunction with the *Neger* and *Marder* concept. This is a colloquialism of the English language and for the purposes of this book I have instead used the term 'piloted torpedo'. This is a way to distinguish the German weapons from the Japanese *Kaiten*, a true human torpedo in the literal sense of the term in that it was a single torpedo that was piloted as a suicide weapon, as opposed to the German carrier torpedo and live torpedo combination. The German concept was <u>not</u> a deliberate suicide weapon. However, it could be said to be virtually suicidal in its use. Between April 1944 and April 1945 twelve operational sorties were mounted involving 264 machines. Of these, at least 150 pilots were killed. The strident call for 'total commitment' repeatedly made by Dönitz (and his commander-in-chief) to conventional U-boats and the *Kleinkampfverbände* – coupled with an undoubted fanaticism among many young *Neger* and *Marder* pilots taken from the fertile recruiting grounds of the Hitler Youth – has confused this issue in many subsequent accounts of these weapons and their use.

Molch

As just explained, the Germans began their experiments with new underwater weapons during the Second World War with two types of piloted torpedoes, the *Neger* and *Marder*. It remains unclear why,

The *Hai* variant for the torpedo with the *Hase* guidance system, during a test (note the centrally located cockpit).

despite the Axis alliance with the Italians and Japanese, they drew little from the experience of these two nations regarding midget submarines. A brief dalliance with the idea of a midget submarine like that used by the Imperial Japanese Navy at Pearl Harbor proceeded only as far as the conceptual planning stage at the beginning of 1942. Perhaps, however, the real reason lies in the simple fact that the OKW did not consider these technologies interesting until Germany found itself in desperate need of defensive weapons whose construction would be particularly economical.

In fact, Dr Heinrich Dräger, owner of the Dräger Werke in Lübeck, had already presented a series of proposed designs for small U-boats of between 70 and 120 tons displacement to be constructed in modules using the same production-line methods as that in the manufacture of armoured vehicles and aircraft. He furthermore promoted the idea of building midget submarines of only 23–25 tons which could be transported via a carrier vehicle to their operational zone and released for use or carried aboard auxiliary cruisers or the aircraft carrier *Graf Zeppelin* for launch and use in a defensive manner. However, with both the Engelmann High Speed Boat and Walter's *V-80* in development, the requirement for Dräger's ideas was regarded as minimal and his plans never bore fruit.

During the autumn of 1943, as we shall see later, midget submarines were suddenly pushed forward as a viable concept once more and a variety of designs emerged. The TVA, who had developed the *Neger* and *Marder* and had accepted their limitations in operational use, during 1944 began experiments on a new small boat (10.8 m) capable of hitting enemy ships thanks to two externally mounted G7e TIIIc 533-mm torpedoes; these were lightened as those of the *Marder* had been by the removal of half the batteries, and reduced to 1,342 kg each, which again would not swamp the submerged submarine with weight and cause unmanageable trim problems on weapon release. This was to be a true midget submarine, as opposed to the piloted torpedo, capable of approaching and engaging the enemy while fully submerged.

Originally developed as the *Thomas II* the completed design was renamed *Molch* (Salamander) and was an electrically powered one-man torpedo carrier. Like anything created under the auspices of the TVA, it used as many existing torpedo components as possible in order to simplify construction, and in form the complete design rather resembled an enlarged torpedo. The hull measured 11 metres in length and was built in two sections. At the forward end, and filling the entire 'nose' section, there was a powerful and bulky battery compartment, which housed twelve battery troughs. The after section housed the pilot's compartment surmounted by a small cupola and connected directly to two ballast tanks, initially so small that they could not balance the weight of the battery. During the first tests, the prototype at first would not submerge and then, after modification, the operator had to abandon the ship because he could not surface.

The stern section also contained what was, in essence, the after part of an electric torpedo, a 13-hp electric motor turning a three-bladed propeller, although with larger hydroplanes and stabilising fins. Instrumentation included an externally mounted magnetic compass visible through the pilot's cupola, an automatic pilot fitted in some test boats and a periscope which was of limited effectiveness as it was forward facing and only capable of being rotated 30° either side of the boat's centreline.

The *Molch* was gradually perfected during repeated trials and the finished design did show excellent underwater capabilities, a range of 50 nautical miles achieved at 3.3 knots (dead slow) plus 50 nautical miles at 5 knots (three-quarter speed). However, if surfaced, the oversize control areas were badly affected by anything other than the calmest sea. A further design flaw was rapidly found when the overlap of hydroplane and rudder meant that lateral rudder use was only possible when hydroplanes were in the horizontal position, i.e. left and right directional changes were only possible when surfaced or proceeding at a constant depth. The deepest test dive reached 60 metres, though it remained operationally rated for a maximum of 40 metres. Carbon dioxide build-up within the cockpit also required the

A *Molch* midget submarine carefully examined by a Scottish soldier after capture. Used from the second half of 1944, it was a single-seater, armed with two 533-mm G7e TIIIc torpedoes.

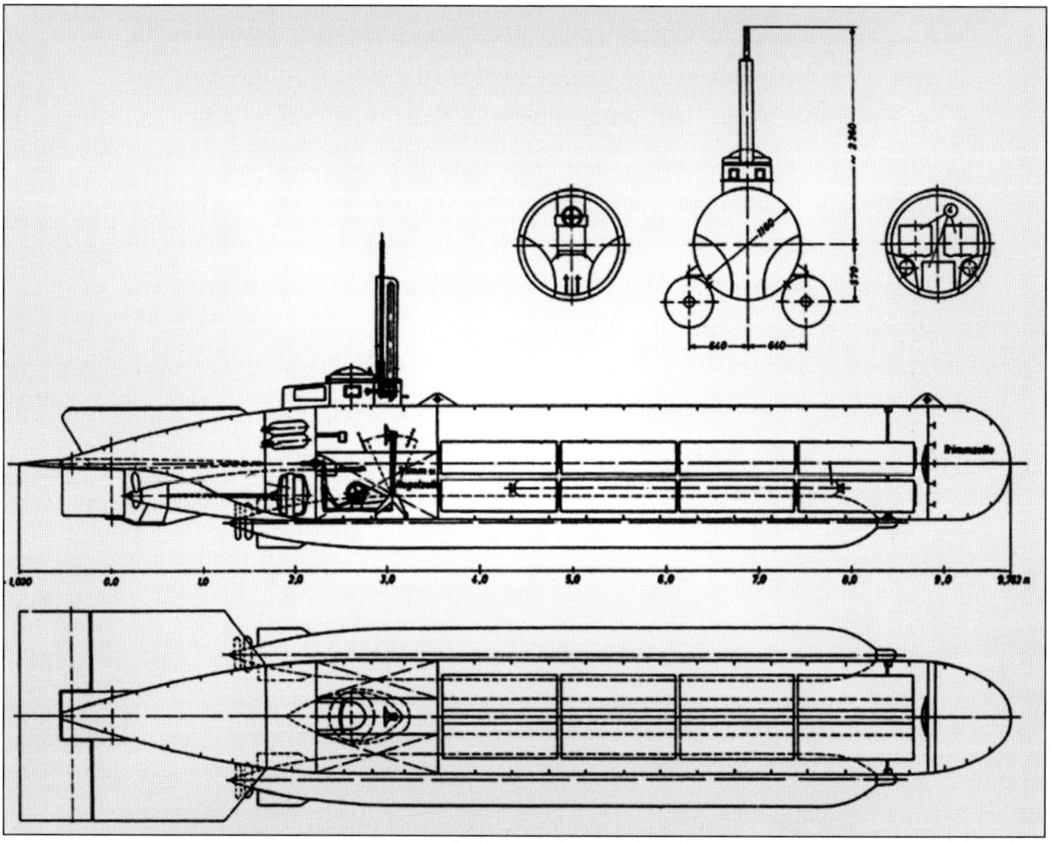

Above & top: Artist's impression and a sectional drawing of the *Molch*.

pilot to wear the familiar face mask attached to six oxygen bottles, without which the pilot would be safe for only thirty minutes. The torpedoes were underslung to port and starboard and were released by the pilot activating pedals. Only a slight list was recorded when one torpedo was fired, though quick trimming was required to prevent the sudden weight loss causing the *Molch* to surface unexpectedly.

The first three *Molch* production models were built during June 1944 at the Deschimag AG Weser shipyard in Bremen and by February 1945 a total of 393 had been constructed. The first flotilla equipped with *Molch* – the 411th K-Flotilla – was formed during July 1944 at Suhrendorf under the command of ObltzS Heinrich Hille and practical training was begun at the TVA in Eckernförde, though later moved to the flotilla's location.

Information on the use of *Molch* midget submarines is fragmentary and incomplete, also often contradictory in secondary accounts. Hille's 411th K-Flotilla had been made ready for deployment via Tournai to the Normandy front until the collapse of the Wehrmacht in northern France led to the rapid withdrawal to Belgium and Germany of all *Kleinkampfverbände* units already in action there. The *Molchs* were placed in readiness for transfer to the Mediterranean instead. On 1 September the fifty *Molchs* began entraining at Gettdorf near Kiel and were scheduled to be divided, twenty craft being transferred to San Remo for action along the southern French coast and the remainder to join the *Marder* piloted torpedoes of 364th K-Flotilla for action in the northern Adriatic in the Padua area, west of Venice.

The flotilla was completely motorised and numbered approximately 400 men, encountering a three-day delay on its despatch to Italy due to intensive Allied bombing of the transport network. The flotilla's advance units reached Capo di David outside of Verona on 13 September, where they were stranded for a week awaiting petrol supplies. At that point the flotilla was split, the larger group of twenty-eight *Molchs* – two having been destroyed in transit – and their support crews travelling to Padua, while the remainder under Hille's direct command, travelled to San Remo, driving mainly by night and arriving on 24 September. While the pilots were quartered in a hillside hotel away from the coastline, their *Molchs* were put into the water and made ready for action. Incorrect adjustments to the difference in salinity between the Baltic and Mediterranean resulted in one *Molch* being lost when it sank uncontrollably within the small port at San Remo after the diving cell was flooded. The remaining *Molchs* were moved to a railway siding where support crews packed material into the diving cells to reduce the compartment's volume by two-thirds to compensate for the change.

By this stage the *Marder* attacks had already taken place and Allied naval forces were alerted to the presence of *Kleinkampfverbände* units in the area. Kapitän zur See Werner Hartmann, a famous U-boat 'ace' and now commander of all southern *Kleinkampfverbände* units – Kommandostab Süd, arrived in person to hand operational orders to Hille. During the night of 25/26 September nine *Molchs* were to attack Allied warships patrolling off Nice and Menton. It was at that point that the pilots were briefed and provided sketch maps of the coastline in the planned operational area, each *Molch* receiving an individual number.

Though the *Molchs* sailed as planned and reached their assigned combat area, the mission was a disaster. The French destroyer *Forbin* detected two approaching *Molchs* on sonar and depth charged them, both pilots abandoning ship and scuttling their *Molchs*. A third, *M-54*, dived deep to avoid USS *Madison* which the pilot had sighted through his periscope, whereupon the cupola burst at 25 metres and this pilot was also forced to abandon ship. All three were captured and, though all the other attacking *Molchs* were lost, only two pilots managed to swim back to shore.

It was a calamity for 411th K-Flotilla. There are reports of two other *Molchs* destroyed by a bombing on San Remo but this could be an incorrect reporting of the destruction of the two lost during the transfer from Germany. Blame for the failure was placed on the pilots and their hurried training, combined with the strain of the extended approach run. The flotilla's remaining *Molchs* were withdrawn to Trieste and then a concentration area at Sistiana. There, they remained until the final days of the war when the *Molchs* were scuttled and men of the flotilla fought as infantry against advancing New Zealand troops. One of the *Molchs* sunk in April 1945 is still visible in the waters in front of the village.

A *Molch* midget submarine on its triple-sided transport trailer (featuring twin wheels). Ten of these submarines arrived in Liguria on 22 September 1944 and were deployed along the Riviera di Ponente, from where they carried out a few unsuccessful missions.

For the sake of completeness, it can be added that a recurring though unconfirmed rumour speaks of a 'landing place for German submarines' on Gallinara Island, in the waters of Albenga (Savona), on which there were anti-aircraft and observation positions amid both natural and artificial tunnels. These tunnels extended both above and below sea level, and it cannot be definitively dismissed that either in the island's marina or one of the small bays there could have been one or more *Molchs*. If it had been the smaller *Marders*, the contemporary eyewitnesses would probably have spoken of *maiale* ('pigs') using the nickname with which Italians called the slow-running piloted torpedoes, and not of 'submarines'.

During December 1944 *Molch* midget submarines were deployed in Norway (415th K-Flotilla) and the Netherlands for operations in the Scheldt Estuary (412th and 413th K-Flotillas). Though the

Molch Technical Details

Displacement:	11 tons
Length:	10.8 metres
Diameter:	1.82 metres
Propulsion:	13.9-hp (10.4-kW) electric motor + 12 Type 13 T210 batteries
Speed:	4.3 knots (8 km/h) on surface; 5 knots (9.3 km/h) submerged
Range:	50 naut. miles @ 4.3 knots (93 km @ 8 km/h) surfaced, 40 naut. miles @ 5 knots (74 km @ 9.3 km/h) submerged
Crew:	1
Armament:	2 × G7e TIIIc 533-mm torpedoes

Norwegian *Molchs* were held for coastal defence and saw no action, in the Scheldt *Molchs* participated in 102 sorties in support of the vastly superior *Biber* midget submarines, but without confirmed successes.

Biber

On 22 September 1943 British X-Craft midget submarines successfully attacked and damaged the leviathan *Tirpitz* in its sheltered Norwegian anchorage. Though none of the X-Craft survived the attack and several crew were captured, they had shown their worth and one salvaged X-Craft later proved valuable to the development of the *Seehund*. Two months later, during an unsuccessful raid on the floating dock at Bergen, the Norwegian-crewed British submarine *Welman 46*, was captured after it had become entangled in an anti-submarine net and forced to surface. The Welman was a one-man electrically driven submersible design, built with relatively cheap materials and intended to deliver a detachable 425-lb (193-kg) time-fused explosive charge which could be magnetically attached to a target ship's hull. It was hindered by the lack of a periscope, and limited visibility even while surfaced and soon found wanting in active service.

Four Welmans had taken part in the raid, none of them successful, as the remaining three were scuttled with their pilots managing to evade capture and return via the Norwegian underground to Britain. The pilot of *W46*, Lt Bjørn Pedersen, was captured and survived the war as a prisoner. His recovered Welman – though considered of poor quality by German naval inspectors – provided direct inspiration for the Kriegsmarine to design a vessel with similar, though superior, characteristics.

Work was directed by Korvettenkapitän Hans Bartels, a former *M1* minesweeper commander and senior officer of patrol boats in Norway. Bartels had submitted a memorandum to OKM in 1942 on the possibility of developing midget submarines for coastal defence and was an early recruit to Heye's *Kleinkampfverbände*. Initial discussions on the new design began at Lübeck's Flenderwerke shipyard on 4 February 1944 and by 15 March a working prototype known as a 'Bunte boat' (after Flenderwerke's Director Bunte) but officially named *Adam* was ready. Visibly different to the subsequent *Biber*, 'Adam' measured 7 metres in length with a 96-cm beam and displaced 3 tons. The initial test was a spectacular failure as

The prototype *Adam* under test.

Adam unexpectedly sank, but further trials on 29 May in the Trave River, conducted by Bartels himself, proved highly satisfactory. A series of twenty-four more craft had already been ordered from Flenderwerke to be delivered from the end of May.

From the beginning it was feared that the exhaust emitted by the 32-hp Opel 'Otto' petrol engine that propelled the craft while surfaced could be harmful, but the great availability of this powerplant and the relatively little noise it generated convinced designers to accept the risk. At any rate, with the imperative to get the vessel into service, there were no suitable diesel engines available. However, it was accepted that if the vessel sailed more than forty-five minutes with the hatch closed, the pilot risked suffocation. This is what eventually happened to *Biber 90*, captured by HMS *Ready* on the surface as it drifted with a dead pilot, Joachim Langsdorff, on 29 December 1944, despite the presence on board of oxygen cylinders allowing 20 hours of breathable supply. He had evidently failed to close the engine exhaust system properly. This *Biber* is now in the collection of the Imperial War Museum. An explosion related to the petrol engine was also a potential hazard: 225 litres of petrol were carried in the fuel tank (giving a range of 100 nautical miles at 6.5 knots). For submerged travel, three torpedo battery troughs were installed, each carrying four batteries, which allowed the 13-hp electric torpedo motor to give a maximum sped of 5.3 knots for 8.6 nautical miles

Biber Technical Details.	
Displacement:	5.7 tons
Length:	8.9 metres
Keel:	1.6 metres
Propulsion:	32-hp Otto cycle engine on surface; 13-hp (9.7-kW) motor submerged
Speed:	6.5 knots (12.3 km/h) surface; 5.3 knots (9.8 km/h) submerged
Range:	100 naut. miles (185 km), surface
Crew:	1
Armament:	2 × G7e TIIIc 533-mm torpedoes or 2 mines

and a further 8 nautical miles at the reduced speed of 2 knots.

Following modifications to the original prototype the production model was named *Biber* (Beaver). Balancing size and weight, *Biber* was constructed with a 3-mm-thick sheet steel hull, decreasing its original planned maximum depth slightly to 20 metres, though it could reach 30 metres. The three-section hull was bolted together with rubber flanges between the joins and strengthened by flat bar frame ribs providing sufficient structural integrity despite the inherent weakness of a segmented hull. The flanges were occasionally prone to leakage and pilots were instructed to dive their boats for two hours and check for water ingress before they would be cleared for action.

A *Biber* midget submarine, with a camouflaged periscope.

The forward section of the *Biber* contained a bow-mounted diving tank and the battery troughs. Slightly forward of centre was the cockpit, with the pilot's chair atop a further battery and crowned with a small conning tower in which the pilot's head was naturally positioned and through which a small circular, sprung hatch allowed entrance and exit. The tower was made of aluminium alloy and was bolted on to the hull, six rectangular ports with armoured glass windows providing an all-round view; one to front, one to rear and two on either side. Fitted to the tower was a projector compass, the

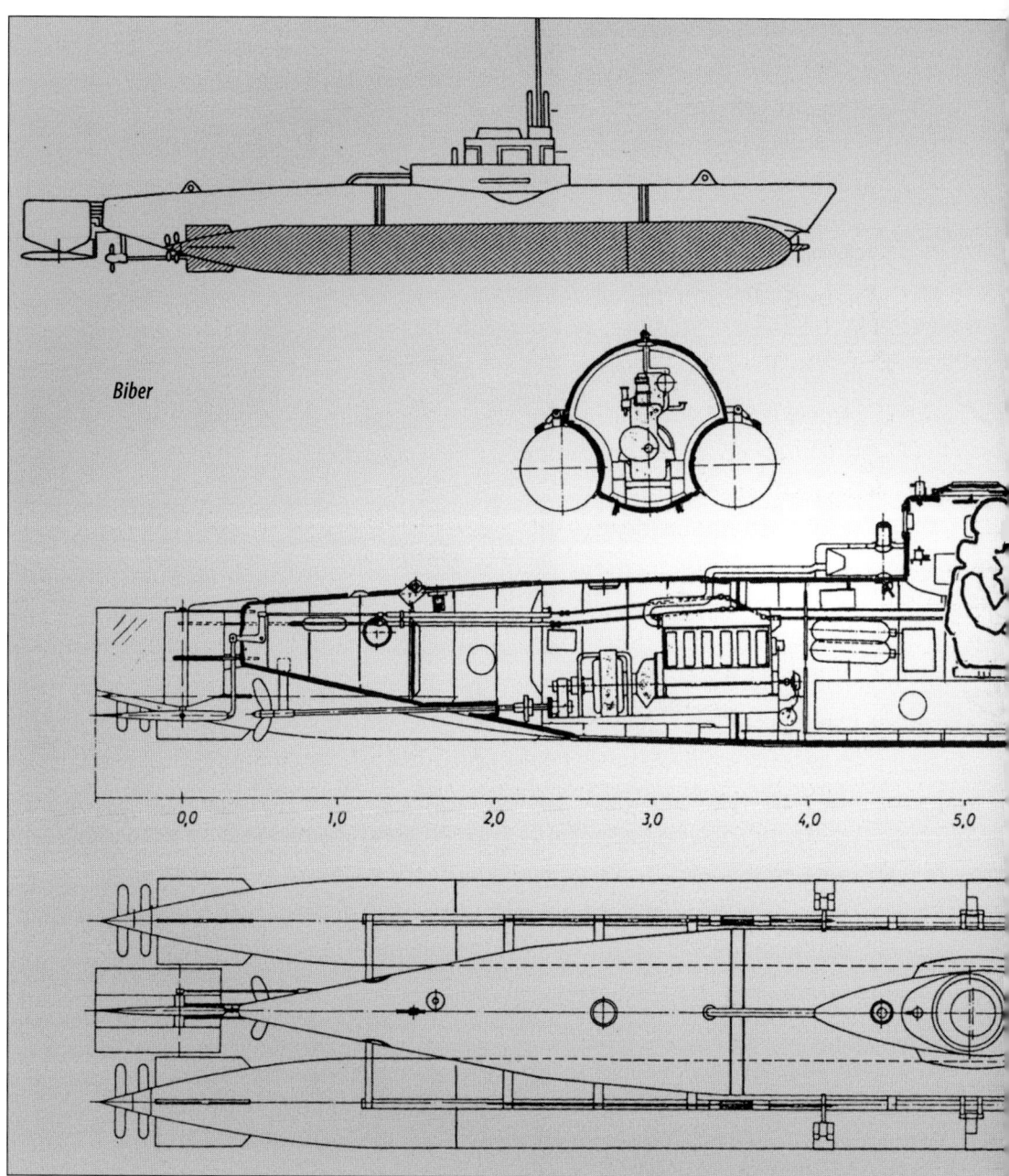

Biber

magnets for which were housed in the top of a sealed bronze 75-cm tube that passed through the tower ceiling. Immediately behind that was the periscope which extended 45 cm above the tower, limited in its traverse by lack of internal tower space and providing a maximum

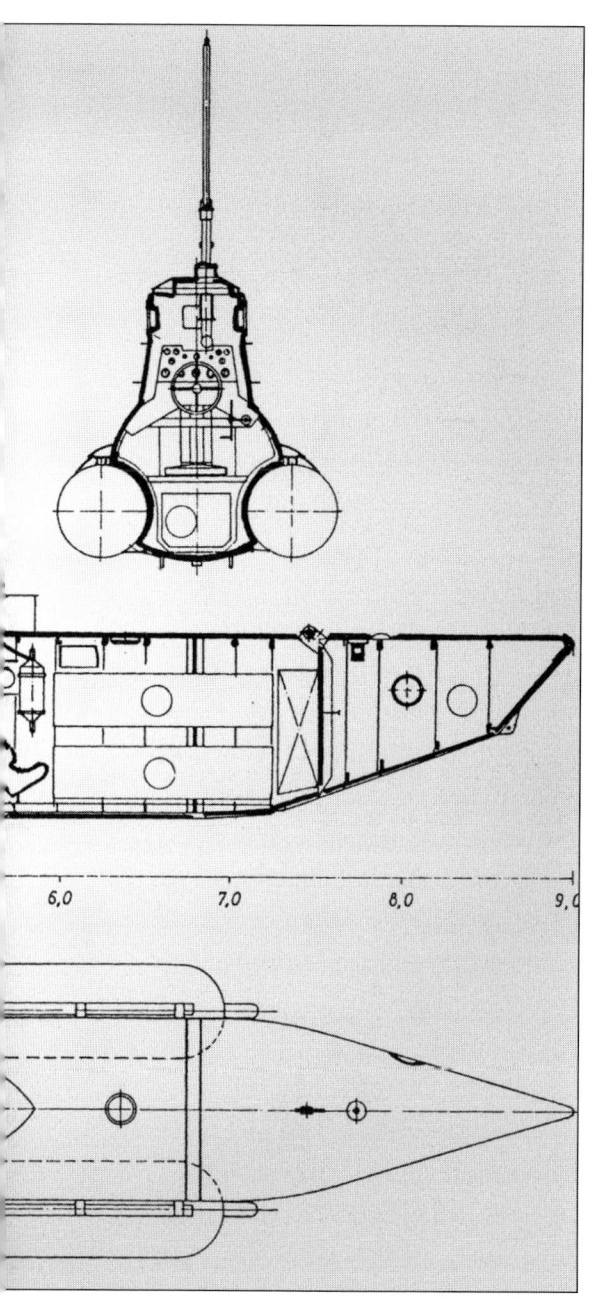

of 40° left and right of the boat's centreline. Behind the periscope was the air intake tube, all three cylinders being joined together by metal bracing. The air intake drew air through the pilot compartment before it reached the engine providing fresh air for both pilot and machinery. For submerged use, a single oxygen bottle provided a maximum of 36 hours for the operator. The stern section contained both the Opel engine and a 13-hp electric motor as well as another diving tank, tapering to a wooden rudder behind the 47-cm diameter single propeller. Engine and pilot were separated by a bulkhead, yet engine fumes still seeped throughout the hull.

The *Biber* sailed on the surface better than many of its contemporary machines, but it was difficult for pilots to master control at depth. Two circular wheels – one slightly smaller than the other – controlled the rudder and single wooden hydroplane. Both wheels turned on the same axis and it required mental and physical dexterity to control both while also monitoring the instruments which included the compass and depth gauge as well as bilge-pump controls and periscope use. Compensating and trim tanks had been dispensed with entirely and solid ballast was stowed aboard before each operational sailing. Therefore weight and trim could only be adjusted by partial flooding of diving tanks or by use of the *Biber*'s dynamic movement through the water. This made periscope depth virtually impossible to maintain, and therefore the majority of attacks would take place while running surfaced, with a freeboard of 60 cm showing above the water. Theoretically, submerged firing was also possible.

The armament consisted of two G7e TIIIc electric torpedoes slung from overhead rails on each side of the hull within scalloped recesses. They were launched by compressed air stored at 200 bar in high-pressure bottles. As well as the torpedoes, the *Biber* was capable of carrying mines, generally magnetic-acoustic triggered weapons that measured between 5 and 5.5 metres in length, though possessing the same diameter as G7e torpedoes, which were released by a pneumatic device, or alternatively by two mines with acoustic or timed triggers. Heavier than torpedoes, each hemispherical end of the mine was equipped with a float chamber to offset this. If a *Biber* sailed equipped with a mixed load of mine and torpedo, it showed a distinct though slight heel towards the mine. Mines tended to cause their own problems as, upon release, a spring mechanism would pierce the float chambers and allow it to settle on the bottom, though not before it tended to rise to the surface and hang for up to three minutes as the air was replaced by inflowing water. Likewise, on release the *Biber* also tended to ascend as the mine's centre of gravity was slightly astern of the *Biber*'s and the bow would lift rapidly at the moment of release, requiring quick counter-action by the pilot.

Volunteers were brought to a base near Flenderwerke where Bartels instructed them in the operation of the *Biber*. The first flotilla – 261st K-Flotilla – was formed in May 1944 as the first three completed *Bibers* were delivered. The following month six more were delivered until by September 117 *Bibers* were completed at Flenderwerke during that month alone. By the end of 1944, 324 *Bibers* had been built.

Under the command of former naval artillery officer Kapitänleutnant Friedmar Wolters, 261st K-Flotilla mounted its first operation on 30 August in France. The unit had suffered losses on the journey from Germany. The *Bibers* were carried on canvas-shrouded trailers towed by heavy trucks and came under Allied fighter strafing attacks as they neared their destination of Fécamp. With the Wehrmacht under daunting pressure in Normandy, the flotilla was immediately to attack Allied shipping in the Bay of the Seine, but difficulties readying the *Bibers* postponed the planned action by twenty-four hours.

By the night of 30 August twenty-two *Bibers* had been put into the water, but due to a combination of damage from strafing, losses amongst support personnel and wounded operators, only fourteen sailed for their baptism of fire. For two hours starting at 2130 the *Bibers* set out to hunt for Allied targets. After nine hours, they all returned though only two had reached the operational area, claiming to have hit two freighters although Allied records do not show any success.

As German troops were pushed back across the Seine and into retreat, Wolters's flotilla was moved back to München-Gladbach in Germany, suffering further losses to Allied ground-attack aircraft as they travelled by road once again. Several *Bibers* were damaged and abandoned, then captured by advancing Allied troops, revealing the secrets of this new weapon despite attempts having been made to burn them. It was the end of the *Kleinkampfverbände*'s activities in northern France.

The problem of establishing a base for naval operations in European territory lasted until December, when all available *Biber* units were transferred, together with the *Molch*, to the Scheldt estuary. Thirty submarines of each type were sent to the Rotterdam base, with other bases at Poortershaven (261st K-Flotilla of 30 *Bibers*) and Groningen (262nd and 266th K-Flotillas totalling 59 *Bibers*). From these locations, forward bases were established at Hellevoetsluis and the Hook of Holland, the first 12 leaving Poortershaven for the former on the night of 20 December under tow by tug. This in itself proved dangerous, two of the *Bibers* being swamped and sunk by the wake of their towing tugs. A second group of nine departed Poortershaven late in the afternoon of 21 December, towed by *Räumboote* minesweepers, three to each R-boat. The *Bibers* were only able to operate in winds up to force 4, conditions deteriorated and all bar one of the pilots aborted their missions. The final one slipped his tow and went into action but was never seen again; three of the aborting *Bibers* sank during their return, one after striking a mine.

Eighteen *Bibers* set sail for an action on the night of 22/23 December and only one returned, damaged by a mine. The remainder were either surprised and sunk during the towing towards their target area, or lost to depth charges and defensive cannon fire; several men were pulled from the water and captured. Yet a single success was finally achieved: the sinking of the American 4,702-grt freighter SS *Alan A. Dale* carrying ammunition, food, vehicles and mail to Antwerp and hit on its starboard side by a torpedo fired by Bootsmaat Schulze. The burning ship was beached and declared a total loss. Schulze later beached his *Biber* but, after compass failure, landed on the wrong side of the lines and was taken prisoner.

Biber operations continued for months, with the arrival of reinforcements and new units, suffering continued loss of submarines and pilots with no further successes. The number lost through accident or operator error – such as the accidental launch of torpedoes – exceeded those inflicted by the enemy by almost four times. This disastrous state of affairs was due to a series of factors, from the hasty, poor training of the operators to the severe winter weather and, of course, the clear material superiority of the Allies.

Extravagant and more adventurous missions were meanwhile being designed for the *Biber*, such as the planned sinking of a ship to block the Suez Canal after a *Biber* was airlifted to the region; the plan aborted due to the excessive ease with which the huge Bv 222 *Wiking* flying boat – the only aircraft capable of accomplishing the feat – could be intercepted. Another was the destruction of the bridge over the Waal in Nijmegen, which had been liberated by the American 82nd Airborne Division in September 1944. The operation, which

Lehrkommando 300 Flotilla Engineer Korvettenkapitän Erhardt helps Admiral Dönitz climb into a *Seehund* during an inspection tour.

Hecht

would have required the use of many *Bibers* and torpedoes, was interrupted by Allied artillery fire, which hit the units before they had arrived at their target.

The Germans had failed to pay due attention to the technique of transporting midget submarines with other larger submarines, despite this method being successfully employed by the Italians, Japanese and British. Finally, in January 1945, after a difficult move to Norwegian waters an attempt was made to use this method in an attack on the Soviet battleship *Arkhangelsk* (the former HMS *Royal Sovereign*) anchored in the Kola Inlet. The operation was attempted on 5 January with three Type VIIC U-boats – *U-295*, *U-716* and *U-739* – each adapted to carry two *Bibers* of 263rd K-Flotilla fixed to their upper deck casing. However, trials had failed to detect the effect of the Type VIIC engine vibrations on the fragile *Bibers* and during their mainly surface transit in harsh winter weather, all *Bibers* were found to have suffered either internal fuel leaks or ruptured stern glands that allowed water to enter after the Type VIICs had submerged to pass the few hours of light. The crews were unable to repair the problems satisfactorily and the operation was cancelled.

With the task-overloading of *Biber* pilots an enlarged two-man version designated *Biber II* was designed by Flenderwerke. This, in turn was subsequently modified to *Biber III* when tests of closed-cycle diesel engines were successful. Planned to use a Daimler Benz four-cylinder diesel engine, the project never passed beyond towing tests of the prospective hull shape and enclosure tests of the engine installation before the end of the war.

Hecht, *Seehund* and *Delphin*

During the Royal Navy's Operation 'Source' on 22 September 1943, six British X-Craft midget submarines attempted to sink the battleship *Tirpitz* that lay at anchor in Kåfjord, Norway. The operation was originally intended to neutralise *Tirpitz* and *Scharnhorst* both within Kåfjord, and the heavy cruiser *Lützow* in Langfjord. *Scharnhorst* was not present at the time of the attack and the single X-Craft designated to attack *Lützow* was damaged and scuttled while under tow to its operational area by the submarine HMS *Sea Nymph*. Ultimately, two X-Craft – *X6* and *X7* – managed to drop their charges under *Tirpitz* which exploded as planned and

A *Hecht* midget submarine, with two crewmen and armament consisting of a single 533-mm G7e TIIIc torpedo.

caused considerable damage. Both were detected after depositing the explosives and taken under fire, whereupon each three-man crew abandoned ship to be taken prisoner. Both wrecks were recovered and studied by the Germans who began planning their own version of the machine, designated the Type XXVIIA and known as *Hecht* (Pike). A two-seater submarine, it was created for the purpose of attacking enemy ships by use of a detachable mine in the same manner as the X-Craft, but was smaller and more rudimentary than its British equivalent.

Hecht was designed to operate submerged throughout a mission, so carried no surface engine but only a 12-hp AEG torpedo motor powered by batteries in five 17T torpedo troughs, three lying horizontally at the forward part of the hull, one centrally above and another centrally below, all reinforced with thicker plates theoretically to hold a greater charge and providing a longer life at low discharge rate. Though the maximum speed reached 6 knots, the optimal range of the machine was only 38 nautical miles at a speed of 4 knots, though if the nose-mounted mine was replaced by an additional battery pack, *Hecht* was able to travel 69 nautical miles. In either case, *Hecht* would require lifting via surface transport to its combat area before release.

The hull form was extremely hydrodynamic and to facilitate the crossing of underwater protection nets or other obstacles, it carried no hydroplanes or any type of horizontal fin; control of the dive

Hecht Technical Details

Displacement:	12 tons
Length:	10.4 metres
Width:	1.7 metres
Diameter:	1.3 metres
Propulsion:	12-hp (9-kW) AEG electric torpedo motor
Speed:	6 knots (11.1 km/h)
Range:	69 naut. miles @ 4 knots (127.7 km @ 7.4 km/h)
Crew:	2
Armament:	1 × G7e TIIIc 533-mm torpedo, or 1 mine

A *Hecht* midget submarine displayed in a museum in Dresden.

took place entirely by moving adjustable weights held on a spindle within the hull, a solution reminiscent of the pioneering submarine *Brandtaucher* of the 1850s. This proved extremely inefficient as the crew were not able to react quickly enough to control the submarine's trim and in later test models forward hydroplanes and stabilising fins at the stern were fitted though even these were found inefficient. There was not even a real diving and trim system as the vessel was intended to operate continuously submerged. The vessel possessed natural positive buoyancy that was counteracted by the flooding of 200-litre compensating tanks located on either side of the forward operator's position. The original blueprint design had called for a vessel with a 145-km radius of action, but with no small compass readily available a large gyrocompass installation, including transformer, was included that increased the vessel's size and dramatically reduced its range.

The crew of two comprised vessel commander and engineer. The commander was positioned rearmost and had the use of a retractable

Seehund Technical Details	
Displacement:	17 tons
Length:	12 metres
Beam:	1.5 metres
Propulsion:	60-hp Büssing diesel engine on surface; 25-hp (18.4-kW) AEG electric motor submerged
Speed:	7 knots (13 km/h) on surface; 3 knots (5.5 km/h) submerged
Range:	270 naut. miles @ 7 knots (500 km @ 12.6 km/h) on surface; 63 naut. miles @ 3 knots (117 km @ 5.5 km/h) submerged
Crew:	2
Armament:	2 × G7e TIIIc 533-mm torpedoes

periscope while the engineer's position lay below the crew access hatch which was crowned with a transparent Perspex cupola.

By the time that design work had been completed, further demands were made of the *Hecht* by OKM. The requirement for such 'harbour raiding' mine carriers had significantly diminished and the vessel was required to be able also to carry a torpedo. Due to the displacement of only 9.47 tons, only torpedoes without negative buoyancy could be used, otherwise the *Hecht* would be dragged nose-first to the bottom. These possessed a limited range as they required significant reduction in battery capacity. The solution resulted in a single underslung torpedo and the replacement of the mine nose cone with the aforementioned battery cone instead, containing

Seehund

A *Seehund* midget submarine under repair.

three additional battery troughs. Indeed, difficulties in developing a suitable mine had already been encountered and designers began to realise that rather than constantly refining an already primitive vessel, they would be better to redesign it completely.

By this stage Dönitz had already obtained Hitler's agreement in a conference on 18 January 1944 to the building of fifty midget submarines for coastal defence, capable of carrying both mines and torpedoes. After the initial prototype, fifty-three *Hechts* were built between May and August 1944 at the Germaniawerft shipyards, though their deficiencies and the fact that a more complex variant was near design completion meant that they became relegated entirely to training.

The midget submarine *Seehund* (Type XXVIIB), a boat conceptually not dissimilar to the *Molch* and *Biber* that preceded it, although far more efficient because of its two crewmen.

As the new vessel was taking shape on blueprint, the man in charge of closed-cycle development within Germaniawerft developed his own midget submarine known as 'Small U-boat K' which never passed beyond the blueprint design, but which hull shape would have a significant influence on the new design designated Type XXVIIB (and later the Type 127) *Seehund* (Seal). This would mark the pinnacle of German midget submarines.

The changes to the initial design inherited from the 'K boat' as it progressed included widening the keel to accommodate extensive batteries, lengthening the hull to place ballast tanks amidships and the installation of a foredeck for a profile resembling a surface vessel. Not all of these elements were retained and eventually the *Seehund* was built as a miniature submarine in the truest sense of the word.

The differences compared to the *Hecht* were quite evident: it was larger, with a shape suitable for buoyancy, and capable of surface travel thanks to a 60-hp, six-cylinder, Büssing truck engine, operating at 1,300 rpm and giving a surfaced speed of 7 knots. The electric motor was a 25-hp AEG that could deliver 3 knots submerged.

The size changes also made the space for the crew slightly larger compared to the *Hecht* though they retained the inline formation, the commander sitting forward and engineer behind. They were also provided with superior instrumentation. An electrically driven semi-gyro compass was attached to an automatic pilot and mounted on the commander's panel. Another compass, a magnetic projector compass within a brass tube similar to that fitted on the *Biber*, was projected onto a plate immediately in front of the engineer who was also provided with a standard magnetic compass. A sound powered telephone allowed communication between engineer and commander if the commander was on deck and the vessel in motion. The entrance hatch was immediately above the commander's seat and was crowned by a 30-cm Perspex dome allowing all-round visibility when closed. However, as with all midget submarines and piloted torpedoes, the vantage point was virtually at sea level providing an extremely limited visible horizon range. This was at least partially aided by the ability to sit or stand on the deck plating of the *Seehund*, raising the observer's vantage point at least a little. If approaching a target closed down and surfaced, two framework reticle sights mounted on either side of the dome showing graduated angles on the bow were provided for surface torpedo shooting. For submerged attacks, the commander was provided a monocular 1.5 metre periscope, fully rotatable but non-retractable. It could also be elevated to an angle of 50° to function as a sky search periscope. Deflection shooting was calculated on simple tables and the entire boat turned to the indicated bearing before the torpedo was fired. The armament comprised two reduced weight TIIIc G7e torpedoes, fired by the engineer after relevant instructions had been passed from the commander. The *Seehund* was also equipped with a basic underwater listening device but possessed no radio communications for any external contact.

Directional control proved the most complex part of the *Seehund*, initial models being manoeuvred with a highly resistant yoke that operated a profile rudder. This was found to produce an inadequate turning circle and was replaced by a Kort nozzle rudder though this too failed to produce the desired result. Eventually a two-surface rudder on a single axle – a 'box rudder' – was installed, though this too was imperfect as it produced 'flutter' and made the commander's task of steering more difficult than necessary. Coupled to the forward end of the steering shaft was the autopilot which consisted of the semi-gyro compass connected by leads through a relay box that operated a small electric motor. A remote control steering switch was also linked to this cable which allowed the commander to steer either while surfaced and positioned on the outer casing or from his seat. This remote control comprised switches for on and off, port and starboard. The diesel was non-reversible, therefore any fine manoeuvring was done using the electric motor.

The *Seehund* carried enough fuel to provide a surface range of 270 nautical miles at 7 knots though this could be increased to 500 miles with the addition of two saddle tanks on either side. However, such long surface journeys were arduous in the extreme. If the engineer remained below decks his area immediately before the diesel engine became unbearably hot. Furthermore, though DIX amphetamine tablets and high energy *Schoka Kola* chocolate were consumed along with a 'klinker-free' low bulk diet, fatigue was common and there was obviously no WC facility aboard; human waste was collected in empty tin cans and held aboard until it could be disposed of. By comparison with surface operations, the *Seehund*'s diving efficiency of 63 miles at 3 knots was deemed relatively poor. This disproportion was largely attributable to the detrimental drag effect of the shape and weight of the two G7e torpedoes attached to the hull sides.

German naval command hypothesised a plan for the construction of 1,000 *Seehund* that would have engaged shipyards of Kiel's Germaniawerft, Elbing's Schichau, Ulm's Klöckner-Humboldt-Deutz and also the Italian CRD of Monfalcone, but with the war going badly in all theatres the ministry reallocated most of the planned

A, well restored *Seehund* exhibited at Brest in France.

resources to the construction of Type XXI and XXIII U-boats. Therefore, 285 *Seehunds* were completed between September 1944 and April 1945; three by Howaldt-Werke in Kiel, 136 at Schichau and the remainder by Germaniawerft. Construction was severely hampered by a problem that involved all German U-boat building: the chronic lack of materials for electric accumulators necessary for battery construction.

During production, better engines became available and so on some *Seehunds* the 100-hp Daimler-Benz OM 67/4 was successfully tested which, mounted on special rubber noise reducers, provided a surface range of up to 150 miles at 7.25 knots. But the availability of engines was not in step with the conversion plan of the examples already built with the Büssing engine and so the improved version never entered service. Able to submerge in just 3 seconds, the *Seehund* was tested to operate at a depth of 30 metres, though it seems that it could descend to 70 metres without difficulty.

Initial training for *Seehund* crews was undertaken using the *Hecht* until enough *Seehunds* became available in the Neustadt training centre occupied by the instruction unit Lehrkommando 300. Training included four weeks of handling the vessels at sea and two weeks of torpedo shooting, though the exigencies of war hastened this theoretical allowance. Interestingly, some men were posted to the *Seehund* unit who had not volunteered, but had been moved from conventional U-boat training to the *Kleinkampfverbände*.

On 24 December the first operational *Seehund* unit – ObltzS Jürgen Kliep's 312th K-Flotilla, later renamed 1st Seehund Flotilla – left Neustadt for Wilhelmshaven by road and train where they were united with twenty-four machines that had been shipped to the port's Deutsche Werke for final adjustments. There, last-minute practice continued before they were posted to Ijmuiden in the Netherlands. Casualties were inflicted by air attack en route, but the advanced parties arrived on 28 December. There they would (in February)

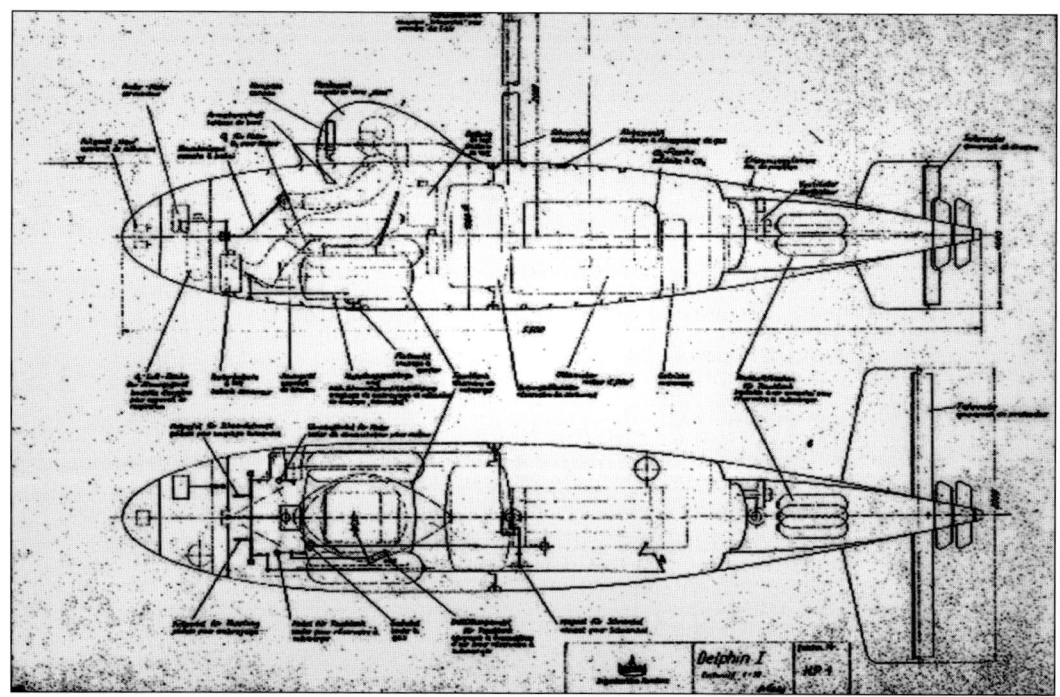

The layout of a *Delphin*.

come under the operational command of Fregattenkapitän Albrecht Brandi, a celebrated U-boat commander and one of the most highly decorated officers of the Kriegsmarine who had been placed in command of *Seehund* operations in the Netherlands. The *Seehunds*, now numbered in the manner of traditional U-boats but in the '5000' range, remained on camouflaged trailers near the port's south lock until lifted into the water on New Year's Eve 1944, ordered to attack Allied shipping off the Scheldt Estuary the following day.

Their baptism of fire was disastrous. Of eighteen launched in two groups, only *U-5035* and *U-5013* returned. Seven had been beached attempting to return to German lines in heavy weather, two sunk by British ships, two abandoned and found drifting while the remainder were lost without trace, one crewmember's body drifting ashore days later. In return the 324-grt naval trawler HMS *Hayburn Wyke* was torpedoed and sunk. Dönitz later reported to Hitler that an 'unexpected storm interfered with the success of the first operation . . . However, valuable experience was gained and the boats continued to operate.'

The decision was made no longer to operate *Seehunds* in groups, but rather to despatch them individually in the same manner as conventional U-boats, and with strict weather-related parameters. The small craft had demonstrated an almost unexpected resilience to depth charges and, almost surprisingly, morale remained high within the flotilla and among the reinforcements arriving. There was sporadic combat action during January, including operations in the Channel and in the waters off Ramsgate. Their first claimed success was a 3,000-ton steamer supposedly sunk off the Kentish Knock, but unconfirmed. Ice and severe winter conditions hampered patrols to some degree.

Reinforced by the 313th K-Flotilla (later renamed 2nd Seehund Flotilla), by the end of January the Germans had claimed three ships sunk aggregating 6,324 grt though all are unconfirmed by Allied records, generally labelled instead as victims of mines. On 15 February, *U-5361* claimed to have torpedoed and damaged Dutch tanker *Liseta* from convoy TAM80 off the North Foreland and

A *Delphin* during a test.

gradually successes began to accumulate. During March and April *Seehund* activity was intense, not without results but also suffering heavy losses. The newly built midget submarines were able to reach Dutch bases from Germany by sea, so the supply of new vessels was seamless. In total, they carried out 142 sorties, claiming 18,451 grt of Allied shipping sunk and damage to 18,354 grt more at the cost of 35 *Seehunds* lost by Germany. The last contribution to the midget war that the *Seehund* made was the replenishment of Dunkirk's besieged garrison with a small amount of supplies in so-called 'butter torpedoes' in Operation *Kameraden*. Two torpedo-sized canisters were attached to the submarine, full of foodstuffs and ammunition, emptied in port and returned full of outgoing mail from the German garrison.

Whatever interpretation you want to give to these numbers, the *Seehund* remains the most successful German design in the field of midget submarines and perhaps with better training of the crews or a timelier entry into the war, this boat could have been more effective as it would have achieved the strategic impact of the commitment of many Allied resources to keep it in check. In fact, even with its belated use, the number of vessels mobilised to intercept German midgets exceeded 500 ships and 1,000 aircraft.

The last noteworthy project in the Kriegsmarine family of midget submarines was the *Delphin*, the first test vessel propelled by a G7e

	Delphin **Technical Details**
Length:	5.5 metres
Width:	1 metre
Propulsion:	55-hp six-cylinder Opel Kapitän petrol engine
Speed:	14–18 knots (25.9–33.3 km/h)
Crew:	1
Armament:	500-kg explosive charge or 500-kg towed mine

torpedo motor, capable of short test runs up to 17 knots by overloading the motor while submerged. Extremely hydrodynamic, plans were made to fit a closed-cycle car-derived Opel Kapitän 2.5-litre four-stroke engine, but this was never actually fitted into any of the three test hulls built.

The *Delphin* had a peculiar teardrop hull built by the coach-builders Ambi-Budd in Berlin, who were also constructing V-1 and V-2 missile bodies. The shape is sometimes compared to that of the modern American submarine USS *Albacore*. For the external visibility of the pilot the usual transparent Perspex dome was supplied to the single operator. The dive control was entirely dynamic. Three examples were built, but only one actually reached water tests.

The *Delphin* was to be armed with a 500-kg towed mine, although early designs called for it to employ a 500-kg explosive charge in the

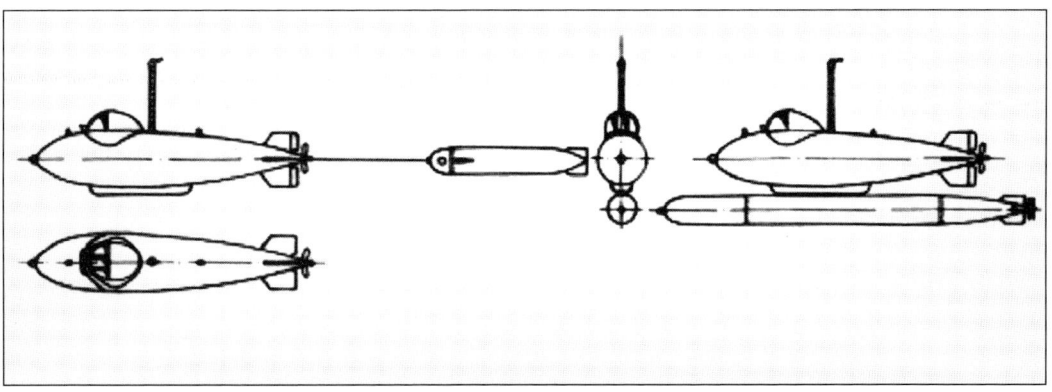

How the *Delphin* midget submarine could be employed to tow a mine or transport a torpedo.

bow as a form of guided torpedo, though the safety of any operator intending to bail out before impact was rated as negligible. The first prototype was destroyed in an accidental collision with another vessel on 19 January 1945, resulting in a decision to abandon testing on the project. The remaining two units under construction were moved from Berlin to Pötenitz on the Trave River where they were destroyed in order to prevent their discovery by British troops soon to occupy the town. The existence of a project for a *Delphin II*, capable of carrying 533-mm torpedoes, is something that has been speculated upon without too much evidence other than provisional design plans.

Seeteufel, Manta and *Grundhai*

While the *Seehund* pocket submarine was being designed and tested, other bizarre hybrid vessels were conceived and developed in Germany, unorthodox not in the sense of propulsion but for their ability to operate in different environments by adopting unconventional solutions to potential environmental problems. Among them were the *Seeteufel* (Sea Devil), *Manta* and *Grundhai* (Ground Shark). The *Seeteufel* possessed characteristics and performance similar to the *Seehund* but was equipped with tracks to make it amphibious, enabling it to enter and leave the water even far from port facilities. The 80-hp petrol engine and the construction of the hull guaranteed the prototype good performance in the water, but the project was abandoned because it was not efficient on land as the petrol engine was underpowered and the tracks were considered to lack transverse

Seeteufel Technical Details

Length:	13.50 metres
Propulsion:	80-hp petrol engine on surface; 30-hp electric motor submerged
Range:	300 naut. miles @ 10 kt (555 km @ 18.5 km/h) surface; 63 naut. miles @ 3 kt (116.7 km @ 5.5 km/h) underwater
Armament:	2 × G7e TIIIc 533-mm torpedoes

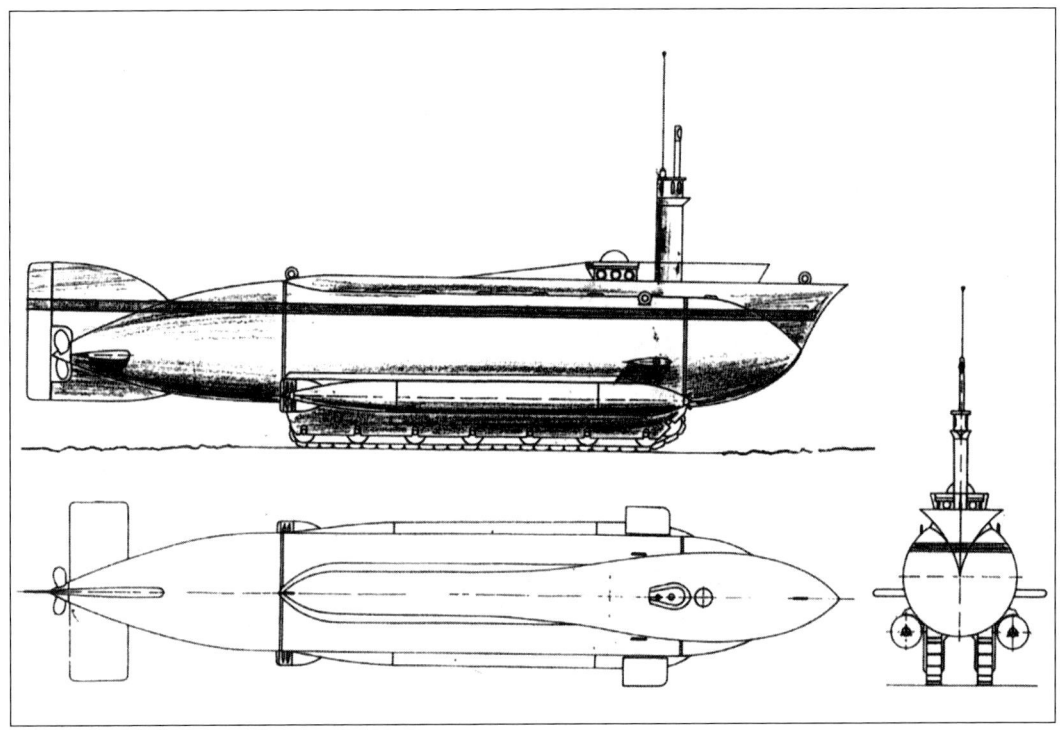

Three-view drawing of the *Seeteufel*; the project was abandoned because land traction was inefficient.

stability. Nonetheless, they allowed a speed of 10 km/h, which perhaps would have been sufficient to enable autonomous entrance and egress from the water. Its underwater performance was, however, satisfactory. The speed achieved by the single test prototype is unconfirmed – apparently 8 knots submerged and 10 knots surfaced – but Harrauer hypothesised that the hydrodynamic drag caused by the tracks would be a major limitation. Although extremely unlikely, it has also been put forward that its use would have been more akin to that of a dredger, a vehicle designed to move on the seabed and demolish obstructions placed in the approaches to ports.

This concept was perhaps more applicable to the *Grundhai* which shared some characteristics with the *Seeteufel* but was designed with the different purpose of the recovery of sunken U-boats and potential sabotage operations of enemy underwater communications lines.

The prototype of the *Seeteufel*, an unprecedented combination of midget submarine and an amphibious vehicle or, alternatively, a submarine capable of moving autonomously on land to facilitate launching and recovery.

Its hull resembled a diving bell but with the stern a tapered cone topped by a large rudder. Towards the stern it was equipped with a transparent dome, not dissimilar (from what can be extrapolated from a few drawings) to that of the piloted torpedoes. What made it similar to the *Seeteufel* were the two well protected tracks under the hull, each equipped with two drive wheels, one at each end. On each flank were small fins tipped with engines, reminiscent of aircraft designs. At least one diver was expected to exit the craft underwater for the most delicate missions, probably from the domed cupola. Alternatively, the craft could operate an instrument inserted above the hull and extending beyond the bow resembling a long harpoon, ending in an electromagnetic gripper capable of attaching lift bags to wrecks. Bow-mounted searchlights and wiring for communications to a mother ship were also integrated in the design.

Grundhai Technical Details

Length:	3.6 metres
Beam:	2 metres
Propulsion:	2 × 3-hp electric motors, two propellers
Speed:	1.5 knots (2.8 km/h)

German historian Eberhard Rössler perhaps put it best when he defined the last of these outlandish projects that we look at here, the fanciful *Manta* project as a 'an especially striking example of how, particularly in times of military disaster, certain designers consciously or sub-consciously lose touch with what is capable of positive realisation and take refuge from harsh reality in never-never land'.*

Manta was designed in 1945 and once again linked to the name of Helmuth Walter. Walter's pioneering work in closed-cycle engines was combined with the experimental units of the *Kleinkampfverbände* as the search for effective midget submarines continued. The *Manta* had a structure like that of a catamaran; a 15-metre long central section containing the crew and two 'outrigger' side hulls that housed the powerplants and propellers and also acted as

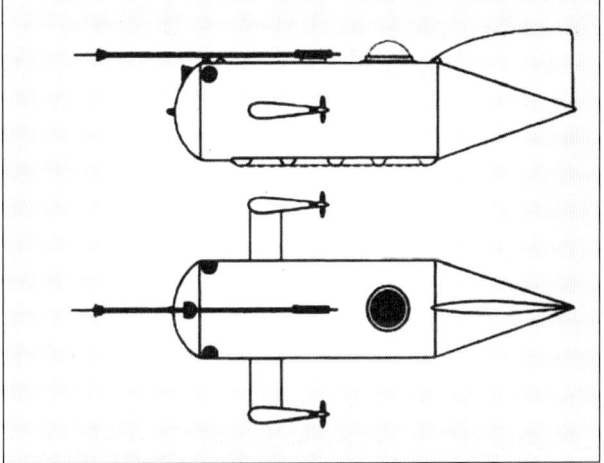

Below: a pictorial representation and two views of the *Grundhai* which, rather than a midget submarine, was intended either for recovery or sabotage.

---

* Rössler, *The U-Boat*, p. 301.

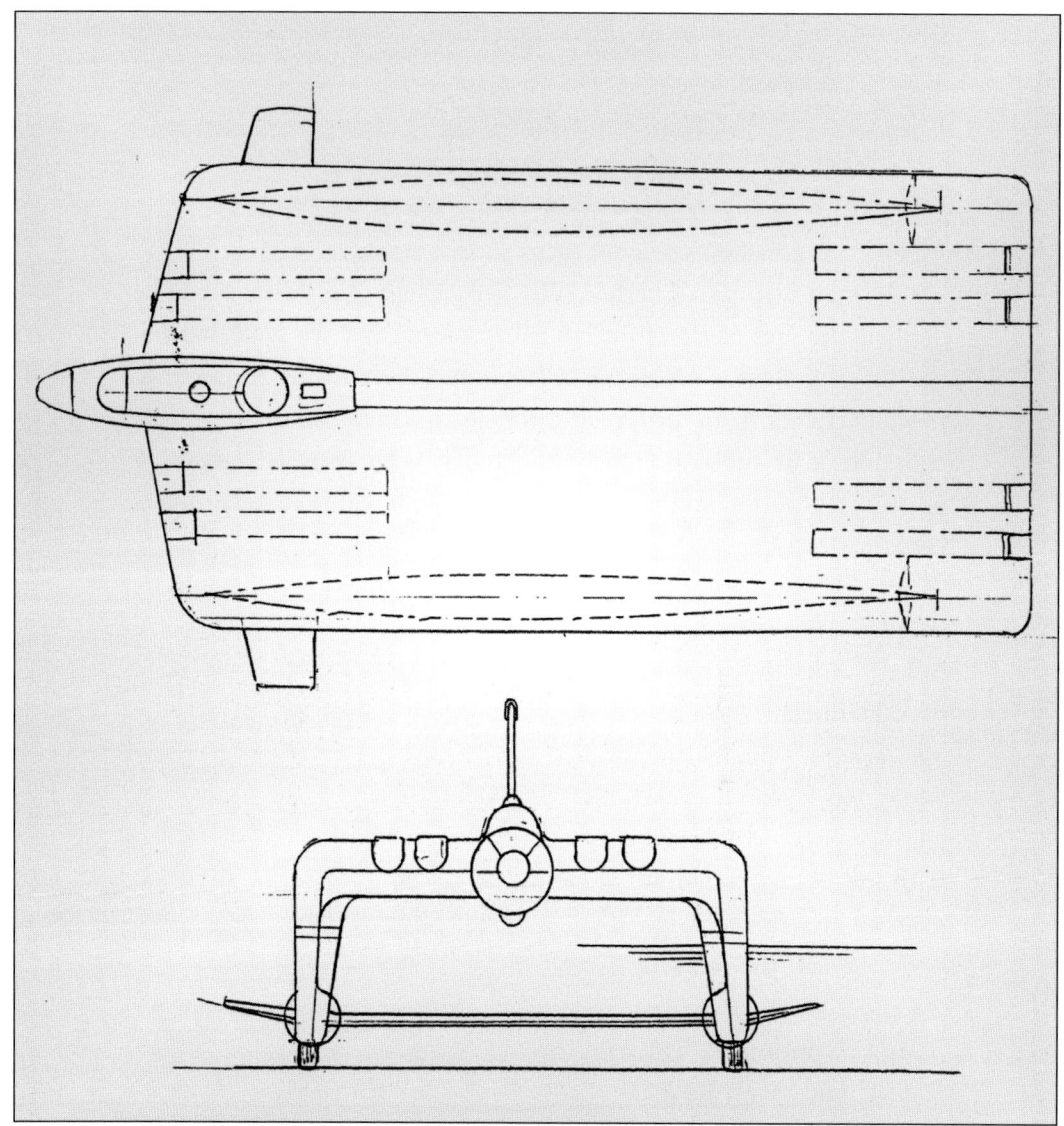

Hypothetical reconstruction of the geometry of the Manta, with the arrangement of the eight torpedo tubes (two pairs at the bow and two pairs at the stern).

fuel tanks, giving the vessel a total width of 6 metres. It displaced 50 tons fully loaded, 35 of which were taken by armament and fuel. Its primary purpose was considered that of a torpedo carrier, theoretically able to move on the surface at a speed of 50 knots and underwater

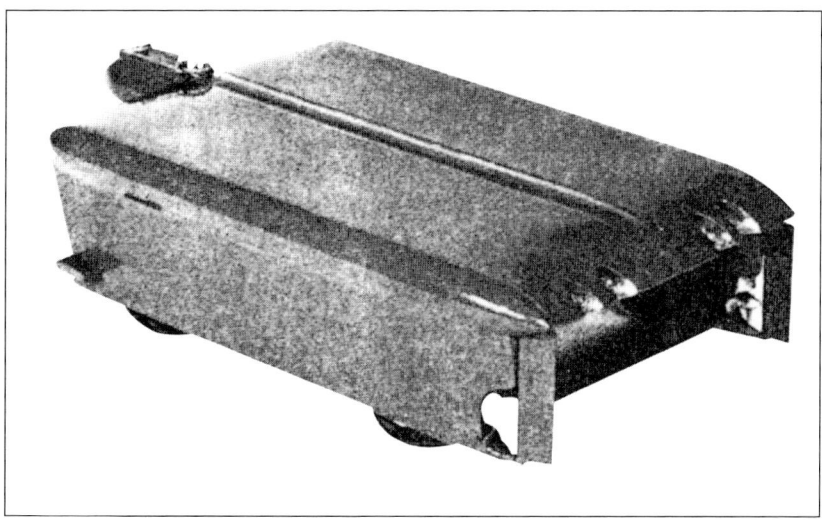

Above & top: Two views of a scale model of the *Manta* project. The *Manta* can be considered as an extreme application of the midget submarine concept, with its catamaran hull and four retractable wheels for mobility on the ground. Helmuth Walter drafted it during the last months of the war. It is not known if there was any form of transmission connected to the four wheels.

at the exceptional speed of 30 knots to a maximum test depth of 60 metres. The propulsion system consisted of two groups of pairs of Walter turbines, powered with the hydrogen peroxide (Ingolin) mix. Its range on the surface was planned 1,180 nautical miles at cruising speed, while submerged it could travel 500 miles at 10 knots or 120 miles at 30 knots. Under the wings that joined the central hull to the lateral ones, it carried four torpedo tubes, which were also capable

Manta Technical Details

Displacement:	50 tons
Length:	15 metres
Width:	6 metres
Propulsion:	4 × 800-hp Walter turbines
Speed:	50 knots (92.6 km/h) on the surface; 30 knots (55.5 km/h) at depth
Range:	600 naut. miles @ 20 kt (1,100 km @ 37 km/h) surface; 500 naut. miles @ 10 knots (926 km @ 18.5 km/h), or 120 naut. miles @ 30 kt (222 km @ 55.5 km/h) submerged
Armament:	up to 8 G7e torpedoes, or 10 mines

of carrying about ten mines. The most curious feature of this vehicle was that it could also enter the water autonomously thanks to wheels borrowed from aircraft trolleys and moved by hydraulic motors. The design never even got as far as testing of its shape for hydrodynamic purposes.

PART III

Major Surface Vessels

Battleships

Under the conditions previously imposed by the Versailles Treaty, the navy of the new German state was severely limited in the construction of fresh warships. Under the treaty, the post-WW1 Weimar Republic was forbidden any U-boats and the total surface strength of any future German Navy was limited to 'six battleships of the [obsolete] "Deutschland" or "Lothringen" type, six light cruisers, 12 destroyers and 12 torpedo boats'. This final class, not to exceed 200 tons displacement, resulted almost immediately in motor torpedo boats, a type of craft not explicitly covered by the treaty terms. Subsequent Reichsmarine experiments eventually yielded the lethally effective *Schnellboote* designs. The first steps of the naval rearmament plan conceived to put German forces in a position to contest control of the seas with the British Royal Navy took place in great secrecy and often involved fictitious 'front' companies located abroad.

German rearmament plans remained in a constant state of revision during the 1920s and 1930s. The desire to circumvent international agreements deemed penalising, the eventual embrace of a philosophy of naval warfare that included a significant fleet of U-boats supported by low-tonnage but high-speed surface ships, and, finally the outbreak of the Second World War in September 1939, entailed continuous upheaval in these plans. During the course of the conflict they were subject to repeated amendment often based on provisional needs derived from the evolution of Allied naval strategies combined with the fluctuating availability of means and materials. All these changing factors endowed the Kriegsmarine with a fleet in constant evolution, yet for all the continuous innovation it proved unable to provide a unified answer to the threats presented by the Allies.

The Kriegsmarine Z-Plan

Admiral Erich Raeder, commander-in-chief of the Kriegsmarine, drew up three different plans by which the German fleet could be built up, looking ahead as far as 1947. On 1 November 1938 he submitted these to Hitler who approved the third construction model that prioritised heavy naval units as well as U-boats. This construction programme became known as the 'Z-Plan' (*Ziel Plan*, or 'target plan'), submitted once more to Hitler after some revision on 17 January 1939, the Führer once more insisting that six 'Type H' battleships be completed by 1944 at the latest. As Raeder himself wrote about this programme in his autobiography:

> The careful studies we made soon convinced us that in the event of war with England, major emphasis should be placed on operations against her commerce, using all means at our disposal – submarines, surface ships and naval aircraft. England's economy required an annual import of 50 million tons of goods and materials, and she was absolutely dependent on getting these goods through. To operate against this lifeline of commerce, in case war came, should be the primary objective of the German Fleet. For such operations, a fleet needed not only to have considerable fighting strength but also the ability to operate over the full expanse of the Atlantic. Because of Germany's lack of naval bases and her unfavourable position, hemmed in as she was by the barrier of the British Isles, these ships must have great cruising range, plus speed to prevent their being caught by stronger enemy forces.[*]

Raeder thus emphatically spells out that Kriegsmarine strategy embraced the destruction of enemy merchant traffic, rather than

---

[*] Raeder, p. 272.

any Jutland-style clash between opposing naval fleets. Of course, to achieve the first, Germany would ideally be capable of winning the latter, thus justifying the persistent hold on the belief in a superiority of surface firepower as the primary means by which Germany could achieve naval dominance.

As a result, following the Anglo-German Naval Agreement of 1935, Raeder found himself in disagreement with Fregattenkapitän Karl Dönitz, the appointed Führer der Unterseeboote (Head of Submarine Command). Dönitz had commanded a U-boat in the Mediterranean during the previous war and maintained a firm belief in the potential supremacy of the U-boat as a weapon against enemy maritime commerce. In 1917 the U-boats had come close to achieving their goal of supremacy over British trade to a degree that would never be seen again, in that war or the next. He would have liked to embark immediately on a large-scale construction programme of the 500-ton Type VII U-boat which was chosen as the backbone of any future ocean-going U-boat force. The simple arithmetic required a substantial number of U-boats: as many units built as possible without stepping over the terms of the agreement with the Royal Navy.

Raeder, on the other hand, preferred to concentrate on assembling a powerful surface fleet flanked and supported by a smaller number of 800-ton Type IX cruiser U-boats capable of operating autonomously at greater range. Thinking in Germany envisioned a potential war with Poland and the likely intervention of France. The chief maritime adversary would therefore be the French Navy as Britain was deemed likely to remain neutral. However, with Hitler's increasing belligerence internationally, by 1938 the likelihood of eventual war with Britain rose alarmingly; it simply remained a question of when.

Raeder, too, was an Imperial Navy veteran of the previous war having served as Chief of Staff to Admiral Franz von Hipper and seen action in the Battle of Dogger Bank in 1915 and Battle of Jutland in 1916. He remained a staunch proponent of large battleships, battlecruisers and cruisers, and Plan Z provided for a strength of 10 battleships (*Schlachtschiffe*), 3 battlecruisers(*Schlechtkreuzern*), 15

Successive iterations of the *Projekt H* design: *H-40A* – over 65,000 tons and six 406-mm main guns, and *H-40B* – 5,000 tons more and a fourth twin 403-mm turret added.

armoured cruisers (*Panzerschiffe*), 4 aircraft carriers, 5 heavy cruisers, 13 light cruisers, 22 *Spähkreuzer* (scouting cruisers which, in effect, were simply large destroyers), 68 destroyers, 90 torpedo boats and an eventual 249 U-boats of eight different classes. These totals included units already in service, as well as those under construction and those yet to be built.

Despite Raeder being granted wide-ranging powers by Hitler to implement this grandiose building scheme, the likelihood of it being able to be realised by 1947 was slender in the extreme. Just the provision of labour and materials in its early phase proved problematic enough. Nonetheless, Raeder cherished his new scheme although in the few months in which it remained in force, the programme was subject to several revised drafts, some providing different totals for the various ship categories, most notably concerning the differing cruiser types.

The new units would have required 33 billion marks and more than five years of work while at the same time, the number of naval personnel would require expanding to up to 201,000 trained men. Raeder had received firm assurances from Hitler that Germany need not consider war likely before January 1946 at the earliest, theoretically enabling him nearly to complete the regeneration of the Kriegsmarine. The more pragmatic Dönitz, on the other hand, declared himself convinced that the goals put forward by the Z-Plan were well beyond Germany's reach and urged instead concentration on the construction of 300 U-boats. This would theoretically allow a hundred to be on operational station at any one time, with a hundred more either training or travelling to and from the front line and the last hundred in shipyards repairing and refitting. On 1 September 1939, when Germany opened fire on Poland and unleashed the Second World War in Europe, Dönitz had 57 U-boats in total, of which 46 were operational. On 10 October 1939 the new construction programme was suspended and, belatedly, attention was gradually focused on U-boats instead.

Battleship H

Thirteen battleships and battlecruisers were planned as part of the Z-Plan, including those either already in service or under construction. The latter were listed in the plan as *Schiffe* A (*Deutschland* then *Lützow*), B (*Admiral Scheer*), C (*Admiral Graf Spee*), D (*Scharnhorst*), E (*Gneisenau*), F (*Bismarck*) and G (*Tirpitz*). Six new 'super-battleships' were to be built, essentially enlarged and improved successors to the already impressive *Bismarck* and *Tirpitz*, particular attention being paid to larger calibre main guns. These were assigned alphabetical codes in sequence, beginning with '*Projekt H*'.

These new ships would have formed the core of the new Kriegsmarine fleet, *Schlachtschiff H* (officially designated as the *H-39* Class) displacing 62,500 tons, compared to the 50,000 tons of *Bismarck*, would have been crewed by approximately 2,600 officers and enlisted men. This design measured 277.8 metres in overall length, with a waterline length of 265.8 metres. Its beam was 37.2 metres and the huge ship had a planned draft of 10.2 metres. The main armament consisted of eight 406-mm (16-inch) SK C/34 guns, produced in left and right handed pairs and mounted in four turrets; secondary armament ranged from twelve 155-mm L/55 guns to twenty-four 20-mm FlaMG L/65 anti-aircraft weapons and six 533-mm torpedoes in lateral tubes. Four Arado Ar 196

> **Battleship *H-39* Technical Details**
>
> *Displacement:* standard 55,450 tons; full load 62,500 tons
> *Dimensions:* length 277.8 metres; beam 37.2 metres; maximum draft 10.2 metres
> *Engine:* 12 × MAN 9-cylinder diesels, 165,000 hp
> *Speed:* 30 knots (56 km/h), cruising 19 knots (35 km/h)
> *Range:* 16,000 naut. miles (approx. 29,600 km) @ 19 knots
> *Crew:* 2,600
> *Armament:* 8 × 406-mm SK C/34, 12 × 150-mm SK C/28, 16 × 105-mm SK C/33, 16 × 37-mm SK C/30, 24 × 20-mm MG C/38; 6 × 533-mm torpedo tubes; 4 × Arado Ar 96A-4 aircraft

aircraft would be carried for reconnaissance purposes, crewed by Luftwaffe pilots and naval observers from the days when Raeder still harboured hopes for a Fleet Air Service. Powered by twelve MAN 9-cylinder diesel engines, four to each propeller shaft for a total of 165,000 hp, the ship's maximum speed was expected to be 30 knots, giving an operational range of 16,000 miles at 19 knots cruising speed.

OKM in Berlin issued orders for construction of the first two ships – H and J – on 14 April 1939; the remaining four contracts – K to M – were issued on 25 May. Only six German shipyards possessed a slipway large enough to construct such vessels and the keel for *Schlachtschiff H* was laid on 15 July 1939 at the Blohm & Voss yard in Hamburg; the next ship in line, *Schlachtschiff J*, was laid down at Deschimag, Bremen, on 1 September as war erupted in the east against Poland. Though steel for the remaining four had been ordered, no keels were ever laid.

Neither ship was officially named; it has been reported that *Friedrich der Große* was one possibility that was considered, but with no real evidence to back the claim. However, in the book *Hitler's Table Talk*, a series of Hitler's monologues and private conversations apparently transcribed for posterity, he appears to hint at potential names during June 1942.

> I think it is very astonishing that men like Ulrich von Hütten and Götz von Berlichingen should have been so far in advance of their times and so progressive in their ideas, and it is a great pity that they had behind them in their struggle no strong and concrete doctrine, which would have given them the necessary moral élan and perseverance. Their completely German outlook nevertheless entitles them to a high place in the esteem of the German people. I have for this reason suggested that battleships or other large warships at present under construction should be named after them. I rejected the suggestion that a battleship should be named after myself, because if such a ship has bad luck, the superstitious would regard it as an unfavourable omen for my own activities. Imagine a battleship named after me having to spend six months in dry dock for repairs! Look, for example, at the very harmful effect the announcement of the destruction of Fort Stalin at Sevastopol had on Russian morale.*

However, this is somewhat speculative because the outbreak of war had led to work being suspended on the two great ships though they remained on the slipways until November 1941 when the steel was recycled to free the yard space. The stated intention was that work would continue once Germany had won the war. Several of the 406-mm guns intended as main armament had been constructed before work on the ships was halted and these were later employed as coastal guns. Initially they were emplaced on the Hela peninsula north of Danzig. Construction of the 'Schleswig-Holstein' coastal battery began there during 1940. This battery was to consist of three of the 406-mm 'Adolf guns' (*Adolfkanone*) split from their intended pairs and mounted in individual turrets. The shell weight for this impressive weapon was 1,020 kg for standard high explosive and 1,030 kg for armour-piercing rounds, and it had a range of 42.8 km for a standard shell or 56 km for a long-range

---

* *Hitler's Table Talk*, pp. 249–50.

By the time *Projekt H* had reached the *H-43* version it had all become completely unrealistic: *H-43* was estimated at 120,000 tons and was to carry eight 508-mm guns. *H-44* (not illustrated) was intended to be even larger.

shell. Their barrels were 21.5 metres long, and could fire 250–300 rounds before needing replacement.

The guns were made operational but the German High Command had already decided to close down the battery and move the guns to a location at Sangatte, near Calais on the English Channel coast. There they became Battery Lindemann, named after the captain of the *Bismarck*, Ernst Lindemann, killed in action in May 1941. As part of the Atlantic Wall, from 1942 these huge guns were among several that shelled Dover, the final shots being fired in September 1944 just before the battery was captured by Canadian troops. Seven other guns were relocated to Norway as two batteries: Battery Dietl with four guns on the island of Engeløya in the Steigen district and Battery Theo with four guns at Trondenes Fort nearby.

As a result of wartime experience the design of *Projekt H* was subsequently updated and, between 1941 and 1944, gave rise to several fresh drafts. In 1940 there were two, the *H-40A* and the *H-40B*. The first, brought the ship's dimensions to 65,600 tons and 282.9 metres in length, with strengthened armour but reduced primary armament of six rather than eight 406-mm pieces in three turrets and with the powerplant capable of 230,000 hp, potentially giving 32.2 knots (59.6 km/h); the second increased to 70,000 tons and 299.80 metres in length, restoring the eight guns and maintaining a speed of 32.2 knots thanks to a powerplant generating 240,000 hp. Neither of these designs was fully embraced and do not make up part of the accepted design chain.

The redesign of 1941 (*H-41*) was strongly influenced by the effect of the bombing of the *Scharnhorst* on 24 July, providing for better horizontal protection of the hull and the addition of more heavily armoured decks. This, of course, made the ship more robust against aerial bombs and mines but its displacement rose to 76,000 tons, ship length to 300.4 metres. This increase in size would have been possible only by limiting the ship's autonomy; a reduction in fuel tank capacity of about 25 per cent was estimated, a decision that the OKW did not welcome.

The *H-41* design provided for the original armament in four twin turrets and a maximum speed of 28.8 knots (53.3 km/h), to be obtained with eight diesel engines, two gas turbines and six high pressure boilers, for a total output of 160,000 hp. Each subsequent draft of the project provided for an increase in size and *H-42* would have had a displacement of 98,000 tons and length of 305.2 metres, surpassing even that of the Japanese behemoth *Yamato*. The armament continued to consist of eight 406-mm pieces, twelve of 150-mm and thirty-two of 105-mm; a 270,000-hp engine was supposed to restore the maximum speed of 32.2 knots.

As is well known, Adolf Hitler had a marked predilection for weapons systems of unprecedented size and for this he was indulged with the design of a 120,000-ton *H-43* (330.2 metres long) and an even larger *H-44*, of 141,500 tons (345.1 metres overall), armed with eight 508-mm (20.2-inch) guns. *H-43*, with the same power of 270,000 hp, should have reached 31 knots (57.4 km/h) while *H-44*, – the final stage of this development – with a 265,000-hp engine should have reached 30.1 knots (55.7 km/h).

By this time, the H-class had become a science fiction project, with four twin 508-mm turrets and larger dimensions than today's nuclear-powered supercarriers. In 1944 the German shipbuilding industry would certainly not have been able to build such ships which, in any case, even in peacetime, would have required no less than five years of work. Nor would the Kriegsmarine have had docks capable of accommodating them. Responsible designers had long since left the entire project that became one more flight of fantasy for the German dictator.

The Battlecruiser O

The same Z-Plan, in addition to the six 55,450-ton battleships encompassed the simultaneous construction of 12 'pocket battleships' or 30,000-ton armoured cruisers (*Kreuzern* P), to be built in a parallel construction project to the H-class battleships. These were to be the natural successors of the already built *Admiral Graf Spee*, *Admiral Scheer* and *Lützow*.

Furthermore, three battlecruisers of nominal 35,000 tons, provisionally indicated with the letters *Schlachtkreuzer* O, P, and Q, were to be completed. In 1939 it was decided to build these three *Schlachtkreuzern* instead of as many *Kreuzern* P. These ships were to have a mixed propulsion system with eight MAN 24-cylinder diesel engines and a Brown-Boveri gas turbine for a total of 176,000 hp. This solution would have provided the ship with great autonomy, equal to an operational range of almost 26,000 km at 19 knots, and the possibility of reaching high speeds of up to 33.4 knots

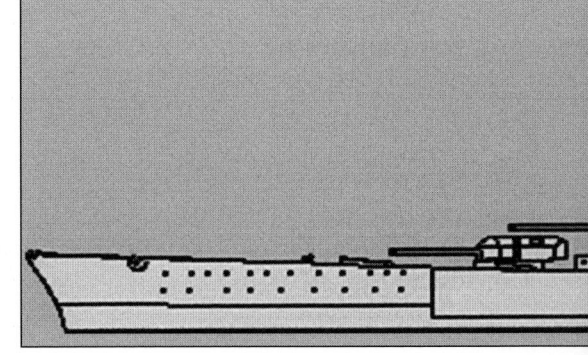

> **Battlecruiser O Technical Details**
>
> *Displacement:* standard 32,200 tons; full load 38,200 tons
> *Dimensions:* length 256.5 metres; beam 30.0 metres; maximum draft 11.2 metres
> *Engine:* eight MAN 24-cylinder diesel engines and a Brown-Boveri gas turbine for a total of 176,000 hp
> *Speed:* 33.4 knots (61.9 km/h)
> *Range:* 14,000 naut. miles (25,930 km) @ 19 knots (35.2 km/h)
> *Crew:* 1,965 men
> *Armament:* 8 × 380-mm SK L/47, 6 × 150-mm L/48, 8 × 105-mm L/65, 8 × 37-mm C 30 L/37, 20 × 20-mm MG L/64; 6 × 533-mm torpedo tubes; 4 × Arado Ar 196A-4 aircraft

(62 km/h). With this performance capability, the new battlecruisers could have fulfilled admirably the requirement of a commerce raider targeting maritime traffic in all the seas of the world.

The armament would have consisted of six 380-mm, six 150-mm and eight 105-mm guns plus the usual array of light anti-aircraft weapons and torpedo tubes. In 1939, only *'Kreuzer* Q' was ordered from Germaniawerft in Kiel, which according to the programme should have been the third unit of the class to begin construction. However, work was not even begun; 'O' should have been assigned to Deutsche Werke of Kiel and the 'P' to Kriegsmarinewerft of Wilhelmshaven.

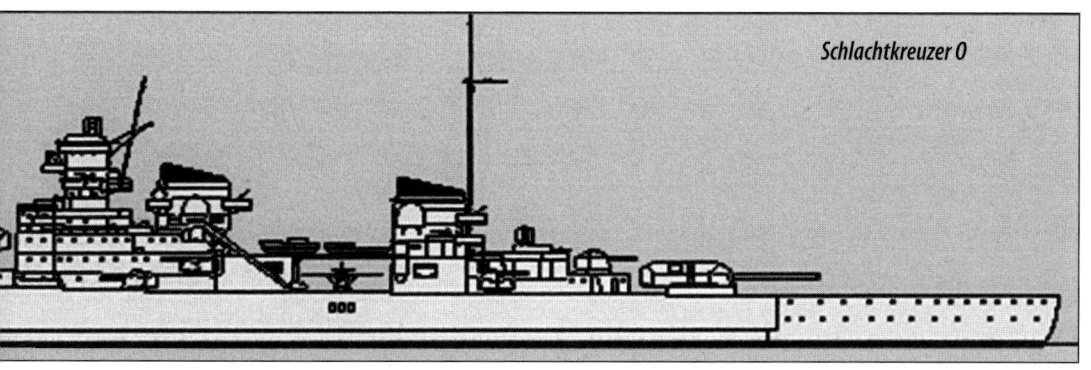

Schlachtkreuzer O

Panzerschiffe P

As just stated, the Z-Plan envisaged the construction of twelve 'pocket battleships' (formally regarded as armoured cruisers) of around 30,000 tons, provisionally referred to as *Kreuzern* P, the design of which was started in 1938. The original idea was to build four units  of this class every year starting in 1939 and to have completed scheduled construction by the Z-Plan's target culmination year of 1947. However, shortly before the cancellation of the Z-Plan, it was decided to transform three units, arming them with the 380-mm turrets already in production. Originally, however, it was planned to recover the 280-mm turrets of *Scharnhorst* and *Gneisenau* after their planned conversion to 380-mm guns.

The *Kreuzern* P were inspired by the *Schiffe* D and E (*Scharnhorst* and *Gneisenau*) and therefore it is somewhat improper to speak of 'battlecruisers', since they were vessels of 35,400 tons. Compared to the old *Deutschlands* they should have had much more powerful engines to allow an increase in maximum speed of 20 per cent although this would have led to an increase in size and weight, but without major changes in armament. Furthermore, the armour protection catered for in these ships' design was nowhere near as formidable as expected and could have negated their use against any stoutly defended convoy. From an aesthetic point of view, the vessels of this new class would have been recognisable by a second funnel, in front of which the catapult for seaplanes would have to be placed.

Again, at the outbreak of the Second World War, the energies of the Kriegsmarine were directed towards the best use of those vessels already available and the construction of these armoured cruisers was put aside.

Like others in the long list of projected Kriegsmarine Z-Plan ships, work on the Panzerschiffe P designs was abandoned early in the war.

Armoured Cruiser P Technical Details

Displacement:	standard 25,689 tons; full load 31,000 tons
Dimensions:	length 230 metres; beam 26 metres; average draft 8 metres
Engine:	three or four diesel engines of an unspecified type, for a total of 165,000 hp
Speed:	33 knots (61 km/h)
Range:	22,000 miles (40,700 km)
Crew:	about 2,000
Armament:	6 × 280-mm, 4 × 150-mm, 4 × 105-mm; 3 × 533-mm torpedo tubes; 3 or 4 × Arado Ar 196A-4 seaplanes

Other Units

The Z-Plan increased the already existing scheme to construct two aircraft carriers (*Flugzeugträger* A and B) to a total of four. However, in 1940, by which time the programme had already been abandoned, studies were instigated for the construction of a fleet of at least six aircraft carriers plus several cruisers equipped with flight decks. This scheme would have involved the conversion of some ships that had been taken as prize as well as a number of newly built vessels, once again subject to continuous redesigning and programme changes which will be described in more detail later. As for the lower tonnage cruisers, the originally envisioned schedule remained somewhat flexible also. Even before the construction programme came into force the Kriegsmarine had foreseen the construction of six light cruisers designated '*Kreuzern* M'. These were vessels of around 10,400 tons, with an overall length of 183 metres and a mixed propulsion system consisting of three turbines and four diesel engines for a total of 116,500 hp, theoretically enabling them to reach 35.5 knots (65.7 km/h) with an optimal operational range of 8,000 nautical miles (14,800 km) at 19 knots (35.2 km/h). The armament included eight 150-mm pieces, four 88-mm, eight 37-mm, four 20-mm, eight 533-mm torpedo tubes and two aircraft.

The beginning of work on ancillary equipment for *Kreuzer M* began on 1 November 1938 at Deutsche Werke in Kiel but, with the keel scheduled to be laid a year on from that point, its construction was suspended on 19 September 1939 due to the outbreak of war and lack of anti-aircraft armament. The portions of the hull already built were demolished. *Kreuzer* N was begun on a date during 1938 or 1939 that remains difficult to specify at the Kriegsmarinewerft in Wilhelmshaven. However, its construction was suspended on 21 September 1939. Information regarding *Kreuzer O* has not been possible to confirm although, according to some sources, work was begun in 1939 at Germaniawerft in Kiel. Even if this is true, during the autumn of 1939 an order to suspend further work was issued. The final two units, *Leichte Kreuzern* Q and R, had been approved and were planned to be built in Danzig and Kiel but work never got under way.

Among the cruisers included in the Z-Plan, there are also the *Spähkreuzern*, so called 'Scout cruisers', which had been planned as early as 1938 and were essentially large 7,500 ton destroyers, and in fact, originally classified as such. This design project was modified multiple times, passing through the *Spähkreuzer* stages 38, 39 and 40. From the last, three ships were ordered (designated SP1, SP2 and SP3 but formally labelled by the Kriegsmarine *Z-40*, *Z-41* and *Z-42*) during February 1941. At this stage the ships were 5,900 tons, 152.2 metres long, with four MAN diesel engines, four Wagner boilers and two Wagner turbo-reducers for a total of 92,000–110,000 hp, from which 36.2 knots (67 km/h) could be achieved. The projected armament consisted of six 150-mm cannon in three turrets (one forward and two astern), two to four 88-mm, eight 37-mm flak guns and eight to twelve 20-mm flak weapons as well as ten 533-mm torpedo tubes.

Following the initial order of February 1941, opening work commenced in Kiel but the construction plans were destroyed in an air raid during April 1942 and construction brought to a halt. Shortly thereafter the demolition order came and what had been built was scrapped so that the material could be used elsewhere.

As we can see, with Germany's entry into the war, the Kriegsmarine quickly abandoned the construction of important surface-warfare units and Dönitz's U-boat-centric strategy finally prevailed. However, hindsight also tells us that it was too little and too late. The Kriegsmarine continued to wage a commerce war that had already been lost by 1942 with a reliance on outdated U-boat types that received constant modification rather than the fresh thinking pioneered by such engineers as Hellmut Walter.

Aircraft Carriers

The bibliography of Second World War military history is now very rich and most of the major topics have been examined and analysed in depth. Perhaps this is why greater attention has recently being paid to 'what could have been' and the realm of alternative history. The first step, generally, is to ask whether what had not been achieved in reality could have somehow influenced the course of the conflict. Of course, this question makes sense if we are talking about projects and programmes that were either not implemented or inadequately exploited by the major defeated Axis powers – Germany, Japan and Italy – since the opposing side emerged triumphant anyway. Historians tend to downsize the possible impact of 'miracle weapons' but surely there is some validity in the claim that at least a small number of them may have influenced the course and potential outcome of some campaigns. With that in mind, in assessing maritime operations one cannot fail to be struck by the fact that two important naval forces, the Kriegsmarine and the Regia Marina, did not manufacture or use aircraft carriers.

Graf Zeppelin

Following Germany's defeat in the First World War, the Treaty of Versailles imposed strict and harsh armament limitations. However, through a series of often ingenious covert operations, the Reichswehr quickly began training officers and men and developing new weaponry with which to rebuild the German military. In 1935 Hitler's government formally repudiated the Treaty of Versailles and announced overt German rearmament with much design work already completed for machinery for all three service branches.

Initially, Germany's expected naval enemy was France and, fearing that French resistance to German desires for parity with the French fleet would once again provoke a European arms race of the kind that resulted in war in 1914, Britain signed a bilateral deal with Germany on 18 June 1935; this became the Anglo-German Naval Agreement. Intelligence sources had already informed of Germany's overseas U-boat constructions and the imminent use of German shipyards and in tacit toleration of Germany's flagrant breach of the Versailles Treaty, the agreement limited the Kriegsmarine's size to 35 per cent of that of the Royal Navy, with potential submarine parity given specified circumstances. The existing Washington Treaty allowed Britain to possess aircraft carriers up to a total of 135,000 tons and therefore Germany could have had 47,250 tons: too few to include the desired four vessels of this category.

German interest in the creation of an aircraft carrier dated back to the First World War. While several ships had been used as 'seaplane tenders', their small number of a maximum of only three aircraft was unsatisfactory for true aerial support of the main fleet. Plans were drawn up for the construction of a flight-deck-equipped, 'true' aircraft carrier, the answer being found in the incomplete hull

The launch of the aircraft carrier *Graf Zeppelin*. This ship and the Italian *Aquila* had a similar development history, confirming that the Kriegsmarine and Regia Marina suffered from the same uncertainties regarding aircraft carriers.

of a 12,585-ton Italian turbine-powered steamer *Ausonia* that had been under construction in Hamburg's Blohm & Voss shipyard at the outbreak of war. Conversion plans were drawn up by LzS Jürgen Reimpell of 1st Seeflieger Abteilung and his final design proposals were completed by 1918. The ship was to carry two 82-metre hangar decks for wheeled aircraft and a third 128-metre hangar deck for seaplanes; all mounted above the existing structural deck. The flight deck itself measured 128.5 metres in length and 18.7 metres in width and the ship was designed to carry either thirteen fixed-wing or nineteen folding-wing seaplanes, along with a maximum of ten wheeled aircraft. This allowed up to ten fighter aircraft and a combination of fifteen to twenty bombers and torpedo-floatplanes. Of course, the ship was never completed as construction emphasis changed to U-boats.

The agreed method by which aircraft carriers could be constructed by the newly christened Kriegsmarine while conforming to treaty obligations was to build two 19,250-ton ships, according

> ### *Graf Zeppelin* Technical Details
>
> | | |
> |---|---|
> | *Displacement:* | standard 28,090 tons |
> | *Dimensions:* | length 262.5 metres; beam 27.0 metres; average draft 7.2 metres |
> | *Engine:* | four Brown, Boveri steam turbines, total 200,000 hp |
> | *Speed:* | 34 knots (63 km/h) |
> | *Range:* | 8,000 miles (14,800 km) at 19 knots (35 km/h) |
> | *Crew:* | 1,760 |
> | *Armament:* | 16 x 150-mm guns; 12 x 105-mm; 22 x 37-mm; 28 x 20-mm; 47 aircraft (14 Bf 109T, 13 Ju 87C and 20 Fi 167 or other combinations) |

to the projections of Naval Chief Architect Dr Wilhelm Hadeler. In 1933 with the assumption of power by the National Socialists, Hadeler had been prompted to design a 22,000-ton ship capable of transporting fifty aircraft and equipped with an extraordinary heavy artillery complement for the vessel type. However, after being asked to downsize to a lower tonnage, Hadeler commenced fresh design work.

Initial consideration of the conversion of warships already under construction to provide a solution to obtaining four aircraft carriers was quickly dismissed. On the one hand, it would have solved the problem of building four aircraft carriers; on the other it would have weakened the line of battleships and heavy cruisers, which amounted to a projected 13 vessels.

Within the original plans of Raeder's drive for a new balanced fleet were the construction of two aircraft carriers, recorded on 11 November 1935 in the overall construction proposal.* Building such a ship from the keel up was a hitherto unexplored area of German naval development and Hadeler was obliged to begin his planning virtually from scratch. He chose as his original models the British *Courageous* Class carriers and Japan's *Akagi*, which would later take part in the raid on Pearl Harbor. Two German engineers were part of a delegation that toured HMS *Furious* during Britain's 'Navy

---

* Berichtigungen der Anlage 2 zu A IIa 3530/35 GKdos. Vom 11 November 1935.

Week' in 1935 while also taking the opportunity to photograph sister-ship *Glorious* during the same event. Of more practical use to Hadeler was an official Japanese tour of *Akagi* granted to a small group of naval architects at Sasebo Navy Yard during the same year; blueprints of both *Akagi* and *Soryu* were handed over before the Germans departed.

Hitler authorised the construction plans of the two carriers, given the budgetary and construction designation 'A' and 'B' and to be included in the fiscal years 1936 and 1938 respectively. The intended commissioning year was to be 1939 – 'A' scheduled to be commissioned on 1 April 1939 and 'B' on 1 October – and a further two carriers were also added as a later product of the grandiose Plan Z naval rearmament scheme authorised in early 1939, but this never gained traction before the outbreak of war led to swiftly altered priorities.

Deutsche Werke Kiel was awarded the contract for carrier 'A' on 16 November 1935, though construction was delayed as the shipyard was already working to capacity, with the battleship *Gneisenau*, heavy cruiser *Blücher*, four destroyers and four U-boats filling slipways that teemed with workers. The carrier's keel was finally laid on 28 December 1936 on Slipway 1 from which *Gneisenau* had launched twenty days previously. Carrier 'B' had been awarded to Krupp's Germania shipyard; the machinery contract was issued on 11 February 1935 with the construction of the ship itself following on 16 November. However, construction of this vessel was delayed even further and the keel not laid until the second half of 1938 after the heavy cruiser *Prinz Eugen* had been launched. Building of 'B' then proceeded at a deliberately slow pace in order to capitalise on potential experience gained during the building of 'A', the hull of which was launched to great fanfare on 8 December 1938.

The ship was named *Graf Zeppelin*; christened with a smashed champagne bottle by Helene von Zeppelin, daughter of the inventor Count Ferdinand von Zeppelin who had pioneered rigid airships. Though far from complete, it was an impressively constructed ship. The control 'island' lay to starboard of the heavily armoured flight

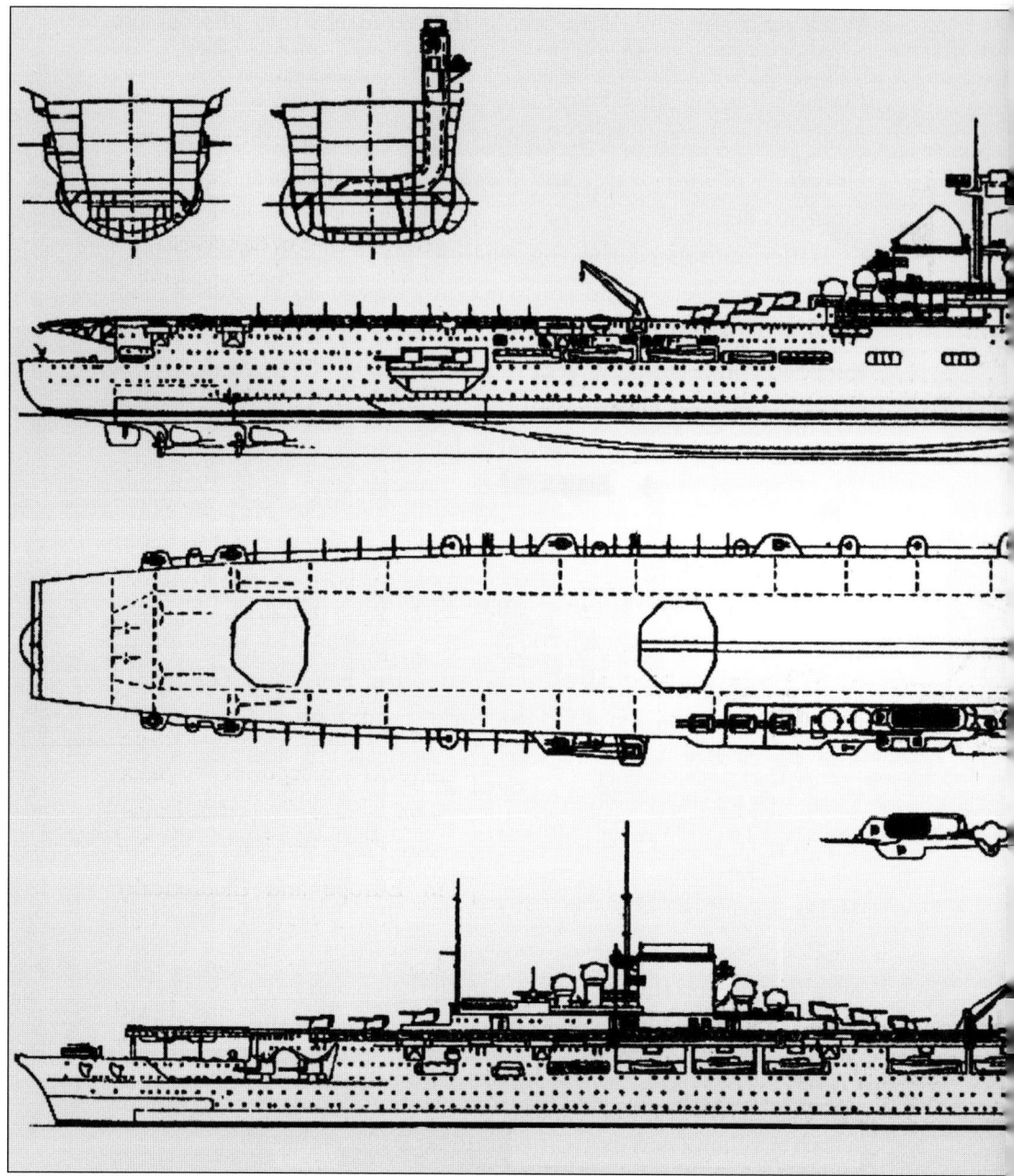

deck, its weight counteracted by the below-deck hangar. The flight deck itself was protected by Wotan Weich steel armoured plate up to 45 mm thick, a 60-mm-thick armoured deck was located beneath

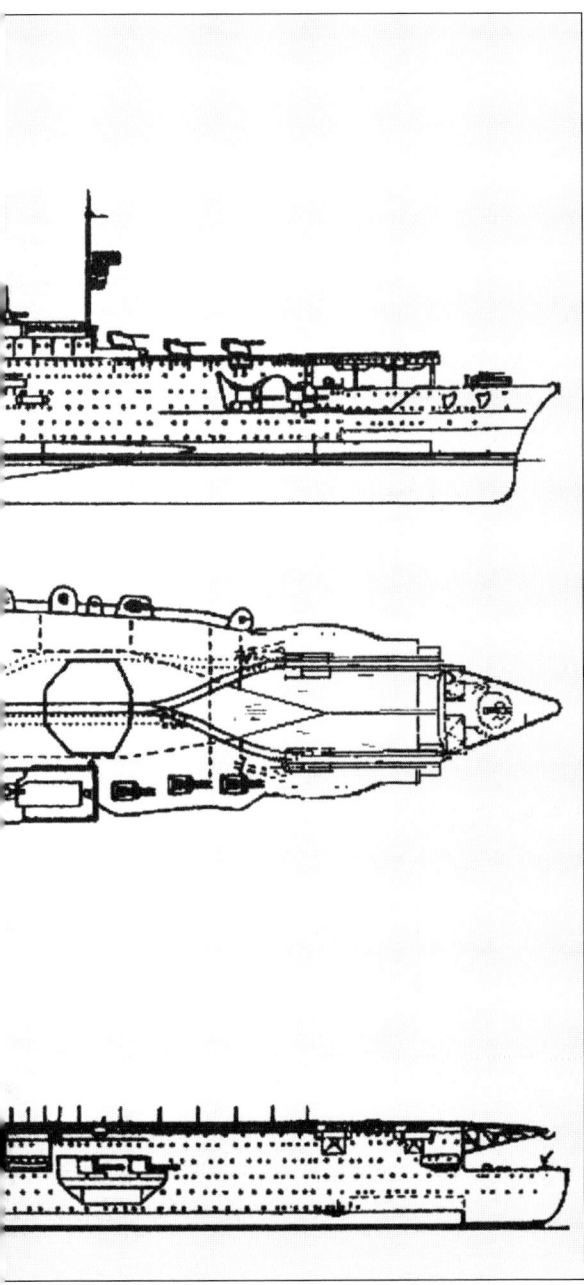

Views and sections of the aircraft carrier *Graf Zeppelin* (*Flugzeugträger A*); laid down on 28 December 1936 and launched on 8 December 1938. This vessel was among those provided for by the Z-Plan of 29 January 1939, commissioned by Grossadmiral Erich Raeder, Commander-in-Chief of the Kriegsmarine.

to protect the inner workings of the ship against aerial attack. Around the waterline, an armoured belt provided defence against torpedoes and reached a maximum of 100-mm thickness in the midships area.

Four Brown, Boveri & Co. turbines – each providing 50,000 horsepower – made *Graf Zeppelin* the most powerful ship built thus far in Europe and theoretically capable of a top speed of 34.5 knots. Perhaps the most contentious part of the design was the installation of sixteen 150-mm L/55 C/28 guns in double mounting casemates. This heavy firepower belies the fact that the Kriegsmarine had requested eight 203-mm cannon: main armament equivalent to that carried by a heavy cruiser. This fact alone illustrates that the Kriegsmarine had not yet fully grasped the tactical purpose of an aircraft carrier, still considering it as a supporting craft capable of engaging enemy warships in a traditional surface action as opposed to an entirely new entity on the field of naval battle. Twelve twin-mounted 105-mm L/65 G/33 and twenty-two 37-mm L/83 C/33 twin-mounted and seven 20-mm L/115 C/30 single anti-aircraft guns rounded out the fearsome weaponry.

The struggle for control of Germany's naval aircraft service between Raeder and the vainglorious Hermann Göring is now well documented. While Raeder may not have fully understood the potential of naval aviation – soon to be written in large letters, particularly by the naval war in the Pacific – he did consider it a requisite part of the Kriegsmarine. Opposing him was Göring, former First World War air ace, possessed of an astute political mind and extreme vanity. Though an intelligent man, his ascent to control of the Luftwaffe doomed it before the war had even begun. By extension, his persistent refusal to allow any body other than the Luftwaffe to control German aircraft would spell disaster for the Kriegsmarine.

Amidst this inter-departmental wrangling, rather than develop purpose-designed carrier aircraft, the Germans chose to modify existing aircraft types, with a single exception. Several types of aircraft were evaluated, such as the torpedo bombers Arado Ar 95B, the later Ar 195, Ar 197 fighter, Ar 96B-2 or Ar 96T trainer, Messerschmitt Bf 109B fighter and later the dive bomber/torpedo bomber Junkers Ju 87E and Messerschmitt Me 155 fighter.

As designed, the ship would carry forty-two aircraft: twelve adapted Junkers Ju 87 dive bombers, twenty Fieseler Fi 167 torpedo bombers and ten adapted Messerschmitt Bf 109s operated by a total of fifty-one officers and 255 NCOs and enlisted men as flying and ground crew. The Technical Office of the State Ministry of Aviation asked Messerschmitt to draw up plans for a carrier-borne version of the Bf 109E fighter, to be designated Bf 109T (for '*Träger*', or, 'carrier').

In December 1940, when the first major work stoppage occurred on *Graf Zeppelin* the decision was made to complete only seven of the carrier's Bf 109T-1s, the remainder to be completed as land-based aircraft (T-2) and subsequently posted to Norway.

An adapted Junkers Ju 87B – the Ju 87C – was to be the backbone of the *Graf Zeppelin*'s offensive power and five prototypes were built, four of which included folding wings and an arrester hook in their design. These were used in testing and extensive service trials, including catapult launches and simulated deck landings. Unlike other carrier designs, all the aircraft would be launched by catapult rather than make a conventional take-off along the flight deck. For this two 23.5 cm-wide, 23.5 m long compressed-air fast-start catapult tracks were installed near the bow from which it was theoretically possible to launch eight aircraft within three and a half minutes. Of the 170 Ju 87C-1s that were finally ordered, only a small number were completed before work on *Graf Zeppelin* was suspended in May

The multi-purpose Fieseler Fi 167 designed for use aboard *Graf Zeppelin*. A promising aircraft design it was discontinued once the carrier project stalled.

1940, and the order cancelled in its entirety. Existing airframes were completed as conventional Ju 87B-2s.

The Fieseler Fi 167 was ordered by the Reich Air Ministry in early 1937, which specified the need for an all-metal biplane capable of both torpedo and dive-bombing, specifically for use aboard the aircraft carriers. Both Fiesler and Arado were given the opportunity to tender for the aircraft, required to possess a maximum speed of 300 km/h and operational range of 1,000 kilometres. While Arado returned the Ar 195 – a derivative of the Ar 95 fitted with an arrester hook and catapult-launching gear – for which three prototypes were constructed, none reached the desired performance standards.

The Fieseler design, on the other hand, exceeded expectations in every respect, including an unusually low stalling speed that could allow the aircraft to make an almost vertical landing aboard a moving ship. However, though the Fi 167 showed great promise, as the construction rate of the carrier itself progressively slowed, so too did Fi 167 production. On the halt of *Graf Zeppelin* building work in 1940 the aircraft was deemed surplus to requirements and the semi-completed airframes finished and transferred to Erprobungsstaffel 167, a testing unit that was used in German-held Dutch waters in research on naval aircraft camouflage. Others were sold to Croatia where their excellent take-off and landing capabilities made them useful army-supply aircraft during 1944 and 1945.

On the brief resumption of *Graf Zeppelin* construction in 1942, the Fi 167 was not reinstated as the Ju 87D-4 was intended to be used as a torpedo bomber; prototypes built which could carry a 750–905-kg aerial torpedo on a PVC 1006 B rack, allowing use of the Lufttorpedo LT 850, the German version of the Japanese Type 91 aerial torpedo. A reorganised aircraft complement for *Graf Zeppelin* numbered thirty Ju 87s and twelve Bf 109s.

The two ships (even though, as we will see, only one was built) should also have embarked support aircraft, such as helicopters and gyrocopters or Fieseler Fi 156 Storch liaison and observation aircraft.

While we know that *Flugzeugträger* A became *Graf Zeppelin*, it has been conjecturally put forward that *Flugzeugträger* B was to be christened *Peter Strasser* in honour of the commander of the First World War's airships (*Führer der Luftschiffe*) who was killed on 5 August 1918 during a raid on Boston, Lincolnshire, when his airship *L70* was shot down near the Norfolk coast by a British D.H. 4. aircraft. Logical this may be, but it remains conjectural and within official documents it was called only *Flugzeugträger B*. This second carrier was laid down at Deutsche Werke in Kiel during 1939 and its hull was completed up to the armoured deck before work was halted in September and lay abandoned until a demolition order of 28 February 1940.

As historians have previously written, to operate embarked naval aviation effectively, an 'aircraft carrier culture' is required and this appears only to have been present in the navies of Japan, Great Britain and the United States. Raeder's misunderstanding of naval aviation would have seen any completed German aircraft carrier probably misused and potentially as vulnerable as all capital ships became to air power, Indeed, the Second World War marked the eclipse of the battleship and the rise of the aircraft carrier.

To this picture it must be added that the Führer, who loved the technicalities and specifications of all large weapon systems, was reluctant to deal with the problem presented by continual contests between his subordinate officers. He repeatedly vacillated in fierce arguments between Raeder and Göring. While the former was a 'stiff' staunchly conservative officer of the Imperial Naval tradition, Göring was a wily and shrewd man of great political acumen and considerable persuasive charisma should he choose to employ it. Hitler would most frequently favour the latter, to the detriment of German naval aviation. The underwhelming performance of major Kriegsmarine surface forces in battle – frequently exacerbated by restrictions imposed upon them by Hitler – tilted Hitler's favours yet further away from Raeder. After Dönitz's rise to control the navy in 1943, this younger, more dynamic admiral received far greater attention than his predecessor, arguably because he was also more willing to repeat National Socialist doctrine than Raeder had been. Dönitz, though ultimately responsible for preventing Hitler from paying off the entire German fleet, continued to press for the construction of the 300 U-boats (against the 249 provided for by the Z-Plan) he had hoped to <u>enter</u> the war with.

Work on completing *Graf Zeppelin* continued at its planned pace until the end of 1939, with completion expected for the end of the following year and by September 1939 the ship was 85 per cent complete with machinery installed, boilers prepared, 150-mm guns already fitted (though their control system was still lacking). However, fresh demands placed on German shipyards for increased U-boat construction forced further severe delays; the aircraft carrier was always considered the least important construction priority behind U-boats and major surface units such as *Bismarck*. Therefore, completion work on the *Zeppelin* was suspended in the summer of 1940 following the severe naval losses in the German invasion of Norway and the need to concentrate on repairs and fresh construction of smaller ships. On 6 July 1940, the *Graf Zeppelin* was towed to the Baltic port of Gotenhafen beyond the likely range of British bombers and used as a floating storage space for Kriegsmarine hardwood supplies. During April 1942 Hitler, in conference with his naval representatives, discussed the potential completion of *Graf Zeppelin*. He was informed that it would take at least until summer 1943 to complete the hull and install the engines. However, more tellingly, the flight installations needed adapting to use Ju 87D and Bf 109F aircraft; about two years would be required to develop, construct and test the catapults sufficiently. Only a small number of aircraft originally designed for the carrier were available and the Luftwaffe categorically stated that no more could be built. *Graf Zeppelin* would require new winches and arresting gear and all aircraft elevators would need to be reinforced to accommodate the extra weight of those aircraft.

> The Führer points out that, in general, the armed forces set their requirements too high.*

---

* *Führer Conferences on Matters Dealing with the German Navy, 1939–1945*, p. 434.

Nevertheless, orders were soon received to resume construction once again, but only for a new suspension to be declared in early 1943. Indeed, Hitler showed great indecision on this subject as, on the one hand, he could not remain insensitive to the attention that the Royal Navy devoted to an effective embarked aviation arm and, on the other, he was aware that a single aircraft carrier, with an aircraft group of 40–50 aircraft on board, stood little chance of surviving the merciless naval hunt which it would certainly provoke.

As this stop–start work affected the ship's probable completion the anti-aircraft weaponry already placed aboard *Graf Zeppelin* was unloaded and used elsewhere, while parts of the fire-control system due for installation had instead been sold to the Soviet Union to fulfil contractual demands arising from the 1939 non-aggression pact. In a meeting with Raeder on 29 April 1940, Hitler decided to remove the 150-mm guns for use in coastal defence installations on newly conquered Norwegian soil. Two of the twin turrets were emplaced by September 1942 in northern Finland at Cap Romanov near Petsamo and a further two in the Finmark region of northern Norway, later being moved, during 1945, to just north of Tromsø.

With Operation Barbarossa – the planned invasion of the Soviet Union – imminent, *Graf Zeppelin* was feared exposed to the possibility of enemy attacks in Gotenhafen and on 19 June 1941 was towed to Stettin, at the mouth of the Oder near the pre-war border between Poland and Germany, arriving on 21 June. The ship would return to Gotenhafen on 10 November, still used as a floating warehouse.

Royal Air Force reconnaissance units regularly sent Spitfire, Mosquito and Maryland aircraft to photograph German ports and, on 2 June, 1942, they captured images of *Graf Zeppelin*'s hull on which portions of the light armament had reappeared. No. 5 Group of RAF Bomber Command decided to try its hand at this tempting target and on 27 August three Lancaster heavy bombers from Coningsby's 106 Squadron, led by Wing Commander Guy Gibson (later to attain fame as leader of the 'Dambusters'), mounted an attack. While the remainder of the squadron bombed Kassel, the three, armed with 5,500-lb 'Capital Ship' bombs with a shaped-charge warhead designed for armour penetration, arrived over Gotenhafen to find 9/10 cloud cover. Bombing nearly blind, of the three, Flight Lieutenant John Hopgood's bomb probably landed the nearest to *Graf Zeppelin*, though no significant damage was inflicted. It was the only air attack specifically intended to strike *Graf Zeppelin*.

Late in 1942 work was belatedly resumed, with the intention of the ship reaching completion during the winter of 1943 and being moved to a base in Trondheim. Due to the increasing threat of RAF bombing, the transfer of *Graf Zeppelin* to Kiel where work could resume at full pace was delayed until 30 November 1942, when it finally left Gotenhafen under tow by three tugboats and escorted by minesweepers and *Vorpostenboote*. It reached Kieler Förde on 3 December and lay at anchor for two days before moving to the Deutsche Werk floating dock where work began immediately on building the hull bulges and completing the engine rooms.

Almost predictably, it was not to last. Following the disastrous 31 December Battle of the Barents Sea when heavy cruisers *Admiral Hipper* and *Lützow* supported by six destroyers comprehensively failed to hinder Arctic convoy JW51B, Hitler raged about the ineffectiveness of the German surface fleet, threatening to have them all scrapped and provoking the resignation of Erich Raeder, which led to the promotion of Karl Dönitz in his place.

Though Dönitz would convince Hitler to rescind his idea to scrap the ships, a *Führer Befehl* ordered all work to cease on 30 January 1943, stopping progress once and for all on *Graf Zeppelin*. The incomplete carrier was towed by tugs to Stettin between 20 and 23 April 1943 and moored in shallow water in the Mönne River with forty men left aboard as a custodial crew.

On 23 June 1943, photographs taken by RAF Mosquitos of 540 Squadron and Spitfires from 541 Squadron confirmed that all activity on the ship had ceased. The aircraft carrier *Graf Zeppelin*, which never fulfilled its original purpose, remained stationary until 25 April 1945, when it was scuttled in shallow water by the opening of the ship's Kingston valves. On the orders of Flottenadmiral Wolfgang Kähler in Stettin the ship was rigged with explosives

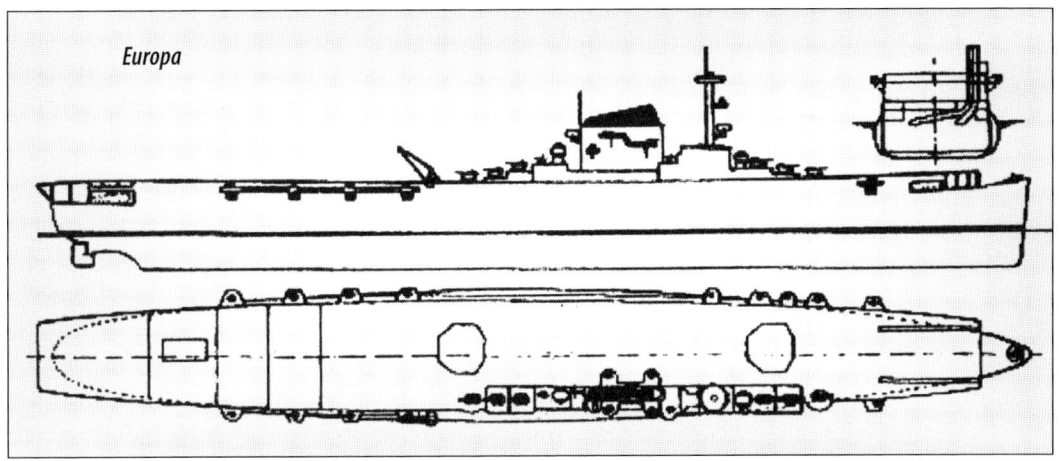

Europa

which were detonated as Soviet troops entered the city, holing the hull and rendering the hulk useless for months to come.

In March 1946 the vessel was refloated by the Soviet Navy and used as a floating barracks (floating base IA-101) from 3 February 1947, until on 7 April it was towed to Swinemünde. With little use of the derelict ship possible the Soviets decided to use it as a target and on 16 August 1947, eighteen bombs ranging between 100 and 1,000 kg were used on it as well as four 180-mm shells and two 533-mm torpedoes, the second of which gave the *coup de grâce*. The unfinished aircraft carrier floated for another twenty-three minutes then sank in the Baltic, about 29 miles (54 km) from Władysławowo, near Gdansk. Here, in July 2006, the wreck was accidentally re-discovered by a Polish oil company, a robot submersible from Polish research ship *Arctowski* later confirming its identity.

Auxiliary Aircraft Carrier I (*Europa*)

Faced with the increasingly effective use of aircraft carriers by other nations' navies, the Kriegsmarine decided to attempt to recover lost developmental ground by the conversion of three passenger liners of the Norddeutscher Lloyd shipping line into auxiliary carriers. Germany had already been on the receiving end of British carrier aircraft and had learned their value on the nautical battlefield in the most direct way, particularly by the disabling of the *Bismarck*

> **Europa (I) Technical Details**
>
> Displacement: standard 44,000 tons; fully loaded 56,500 tons
> Dimensions: length 291.5 metres; beam 37 metres; average draft 10.3 metres
> Engine: 4 × Blohm & Voss steam turbines, total 100,000 hp
> Speed: 26.5 knots (49 km/h)
> Range: 5,000 naut. miles (9,300 km) @ 26.5 knots (49 km/h), 10,000 naut. miles (19,000 km) @ 19 knots (35 km/h)
> Armament: 12 × 105mm, 20 × 37 mm, 28–36 × 20mm; 42 aircraft (24 Bf 109T, 18 Ju 87E)

by Swordfish aircraft from HMS *Ark Royal* and its subsequent destruction in May 1941. The value of aerial support for large units at sea had been starkly illustrated.

On 13 May 1942, in conference with Albert Speer, Vizeadmiral Theodor Kranke (C-in-C Navy Representative at Führer Headquarters) and Konteradmiral Gustav Kleikamp, Hitler declared that *Europa*, *Potsdam* and *Gneisenau* should be converted into auxiliary aircraft carriers:

> The Military Problems and Shipyards Branch, Naval Construction Division, expects to have the plans ready in three months and the converted ships should be completed about twelve months from the time the necessary material is available. The Führer considers it entirely out of the question for larger surface forces to operate without aircraft protection.*

The 56,492-ton liner *Europa* had been launched on 16 August 1928 and after completion – including repair to damage inflicted by an accidental fire in its Hamburg Blohm & Voss equipment dock – entered service to work the transatlantic route to New York. On its maiden voyage in March 1930 the ship won the Blue Riband, the unofficial record for the highest-speed Atlantic crossing. It was this speed that made it an ideal candidate for conversion to military

---

* *Führer Conferences on Matters Dealing with the German Navy, 1939-1945*, p. 465.

purposes, operating alongside *Tirpitz* or *Hipper*-class cruisers. The ship became inactive with the outbreak of war, although it had been considered for use as a troop carrier during the planned invasion of Great Britain. Requisitioned by the Kriegsmarine in 1939, *Europa* served a period of time as a floating barracks for U-boat personnel. When earmarked for conversion to an aircraft carrier, *Europa* would have dwarfed even *Graf Zeppelin* and was redesignated 'Auxiliary Aircraft Carrier I'.

The other two liners chosen were considerably smaller than *Europa*: 17,528-grt SS *Potsdam* launched from Blohm & Voss on 16 January 1935 and 18,160-grt SS *Gneisenau* from Deschimag in Bremen on 17 May that same year. Both ships sailed the Far East routes from Hamburg and Bremen respectively; *Potsdam* was actually en route to the United States at the outbreak of war and was rerouted north of Scotland back to Germany where the Kriegsmarine requisitioned it as a barracks ship, stationed in Hamburg. *Gneisenau* was also destined for use as naval accommodation. The two ships were renamed as planning got under way, *Potsdam* becoming *Elbe* and *Gneisenau* redesignated *Jade*; the pair were subsequently frequently referred to as '*Jade*-class' ships.

Plans for conversion work on all three liners were drawn up immediately, and the enormity of the task was finally revealed to

---

Gneiseau (*Jade*) and Potsdam (*Elbe*); *Jade*-class Technical Details

Displacement:	standard 18,160 tons (*Jade*), 17,527 tons (*Elbe*)
Dimensions:	length 203 metres overall
Beam:	22.6 metres hull; 27 metres flight deck
Draft:	8.85 metres at full load.
Engine:	2 × Deschimag steam turbines (*Jade*); two electric motors (*Elbe*), two propeller shafts, for a total of 26,000 hp
Speed:	19 knots (35 km/h)
Range:	9,000 miles (17,000 km) @ 19 knots (35 km/h)
Crew:	883–900
Armament:	8 × 105mm, 12 × 37mm, 24–32 × 20mm; 24 aircraft (12 Bf 109T, 12 Ju 87E), two catapults

naval designers. They had clearly underestimated the work required and discovered that, built for completely different purposes, the shape, internal subdivisions and weight stability of the ships were insufficient for their new role. For *Europa* an early problem was the location of the hangar: the only solution to avoid structural weakness seemed to be to integrate it into the main deck. It was initially believed that stability problems in all three could be mastered by applying belts of cement formed into 'armour plates' and the addition of side bulges, but both changes also brought complex design problems and, even if successful, would further lower the ships' speed thus negating their primary asset: the ability to operate alongside fast capital ships.

Further complicating the task, during June 1942, the incomplete heavy cruiser *Seydlitz* (*Hipper*-class) was added to the auxiliary carrier list. There were to have been five ships of this cruiser class – *Admiral Hipper*, *Blücher*, *Prinz Eugen*, *Seydlitz* and *Lützow* – though only three were completed and saw action. *Lützow* was sold to the Soviet Union as an incomplete construction during 1940 for the sum of 150 million Reichsmarks, nearly double the original cost of the vessel. Renamed 'L' for transfer to the Soviet Union, the name *Lützow* was then bestowed on the pocket battleship *Deutschland* following fears of the potential blow to morale if a vessel carrying the country's name was sunk. *Blücher* was sunk during the 1940 invasion of Norway; *Admiral Hipper* was finally scuttled in May 1945; *Prinz Eugen* survived the war.

Seydlitz (*Weser*) Technical Details

Displacement:	standard 16,170 tons; fully loaded 18,500 tons
Dimensions:	length 202.8 metres overall; beam 21.3 metres hull, 30 metres flight deck; draft: 7.9 m
Engine:	3 × Deschimag and/or Blohm & Voss steam turbines, three propeller shafts, 132,000 hp
Speed:	32 knots (59 km/h)
Range:	6,500 naut. miles (12,040 km) @ 19 knots (35 km/h)
Armament:	10 × 105-mm, 10 × 37-mm; 24 × 20-mm; 20 aircraft (10 Bf 109T, 10 Ju 87E)

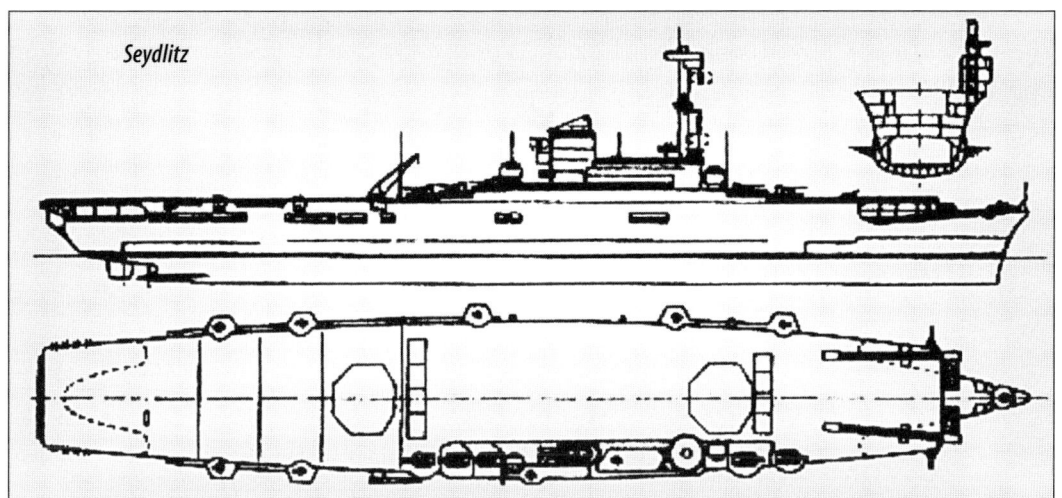

Seydlitz

The design of *Seydlitz* and the other *Hipper*-class ships was very similar to that of the *Scharnhorst*-class battleships, though reduced in, and this explains how, when such ships were sighted at a great distance, it proved difficult to distinguish them from their contemporaries. In the eternal conflict between autonomy and speed, speed was given a higher priority with these cruisers which each had 12 boilers connected to three turbo-reducers. These supplied a designed 132,000 hp (133,631 during *Admiral Hipper*'s trials) and an excellent top speed of 32.5 knots. Range, on the other hand, 6,500 miles (12,040 km) at 17 knots (31 km/h), did not meet expectations: the designers had anticipated between 6,800 and 8,000 miles at higher speeds. The ships had efficient protection (70–80 mm of lateral belt, with turret armour 105 mm thick) and hull bulges that would help preserve stability and buoyancy even in the event of extensive damage. The armament, in addition to the four twin Krupp 203-mm SK/C34 guns, included another six 105-mm SK C/33 guns in twin turrets, twelve 37-mm SK C/30, and eight 20-mm Flak 38 anti-aircraft guns.

When its construction as a cruiser was stopped, the main weapons from *Seydlitz* were dismounted and emplaced as coastal guns on the Atlantic Wall. Though it was by then 95 per cent complete, the majority of the ship's superstructure with the exception of the funnel would be cut away in preparation for the installation of flight deck and hangars.

The last vessel added to the list of aircraft carrier conversions was the incomplete hull of the captured French anti-aircraft cruiser *De Grasse*. This ship was added to the list on 26 August 1942 as it lay abandoned on a slipway in Saint Nazaire. Work on *De Grasse* was soon halted, however. There were too few workmen available in Lorient and the ship had a problematic propulsion system amongst other design flaws. *De Grasse* had been intended to carry eleven fighters and twelve bombers.

The complement of the other auxiliary carriers had, in the meantime, been finalised at forty-six bombers and fifty-four fighters distributed thus: *Europa*, eighteen bombers, twenty-four fighters; *Potsdam*, eight bombers and twelve fighters; *Gneisenau*, eight bombers and twelve fighters and *Seydlitz*, twelve bombers and six fighters.

Europa was to be rebuilt by Hamburg's Blohm & Voss yard, though by November 1942 planning had been halted and the order was eventually cancelled before any work had begun. The smaller *Potsdam* and *Gneisenau* were to be handled by the Howaldt Werke and Wilhelmshaven naval shipyard respectively, though cancellation of the *Europa* conversion led to *Potsdam* (redesignated *Jade*) being passed to Blohm & Voss.

If they had been finished, they would have made impressive vessels, particularly *Europa*. The design for Auxiliary Aircraft Carrier I showed a vessel 280 metres long at the waterline, and 291.5 metres overall: about 30 metres longer than the *Graf Zeppelin*. The initial planned beam was 31 metres, the addition of stabilising bulges increasing it to 37 metres. The initial draft of 8.5 metres would have increased to 10.3 by the end of the conversion. Displacement was calculated at 44,000 tons standard and 56,500 tons full load. The hull was divided into 16 watertight compartments and equipped with a double bottom.

The flight deck was 276 metres long and 30 metres wide. The single hangar measured 216 metres in length, 25 in width towards the bow, 30 towards the stern and it was planned to embark eighteen

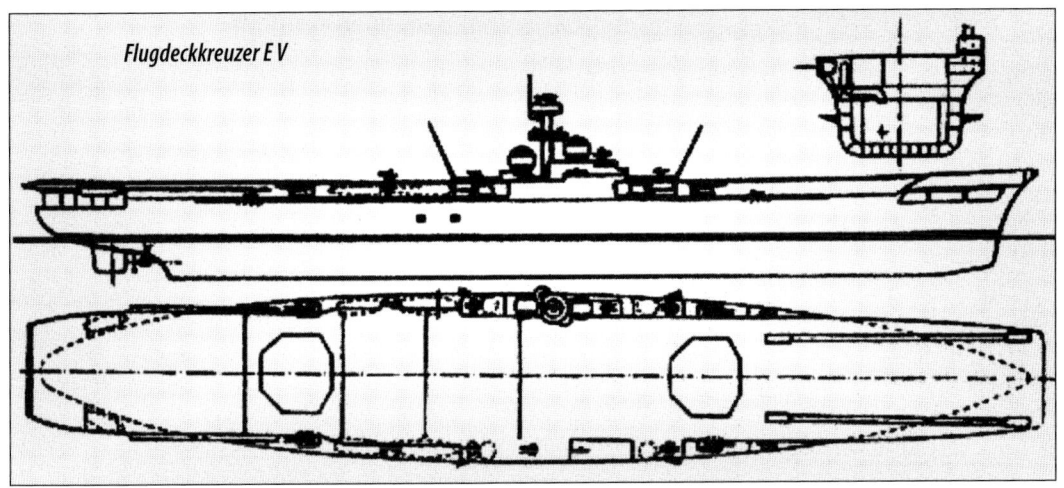

Flugdeckkreuzer: A projected design that combined the raiding power of a cruiser with a full carrier flight deck.

Ju 87E Stuka dive bombers, with catapult-launch capabilities and arrester hook, and twenty-four Bf 109T, derived from the E version but with a greater wingspan for a shorter take-off.

The ship did possess a number of flaws, however, included in which was its lack of armour and having only a single rudder. The engine room held four Blohm & Voss turbines, each driving its own shaft fitted with a four-blade 5-m diameter propeller. The engine was supposed to develop a total of 100,000 hp and provide the aircraft carrier with a speed of 26.5 knots; at top speed range was to be 5,000 nautical miles which doubled at a cruising speed of 19 knots. The intended fuel storage capacity was 6,500–8,500 tons.

Electricity requirements were guaranteed by four diesel generators, plus two for emergencies, for a total output of 2,280 kW at 230 V. The planned defensive armament consisted of 12 × 105-mm L/65 anti-aircraft guns in six twin turrets, three at the bow and three at the stern of the superstructure (consisting of an island and a funnel). These guns had an elevation of 80° and were capable of hitting a target in flight up to an altitude of 12,500 metres. When used against surface targets, the maximum range was 17,700 metres with an elevation of 45°. Each weapon had 400 rounds, with a choice of 58.4-kg armour-piercing or 51.8-kg incendiary ammunition. The secondary anti-aircraft armament was made up of twenty 37-mm, also in twin turrets. These weapons were placed along the sides of the flight deck with 40,000 rounds of ammunition in total, with a rate of fire of 30 rounds per gun per minute and a muzzle velocity of 1,000 m/s. Elevation of up to 85° offered a maximum range of 6,800 metres against flying targets, reduced to 4,800 metres during the use of tracer shells. A third battery of 20-mm pieces (28 or 36, in quadruple mounts) completed the defensive armament with a practical rate of fire of 200 rounds per mounting per minute and a total ammunition reserve of 72,000 rounds.

The other two Norddeutscher Lloyd ships were found to hold the same design problems as *Europa*. Initially, the insertion of concrete counterweights in the bottom of the hull was the suggested method of increasing stability. However, the result was particularly unconvincing for *Gneisenau* and its conversion into the aircraft carrier *Jade* was abandoned on 25 November 1942. Design work on *Potsdam* – now aircraft carrier *Elbe* – continued after the decision was taken to transform the ship into a training aircraft carrier, with adoption of a completely different stabilisation method. This ship was planned to have an additional outer hull around the original one. Work began on dismantling passenger cabins in December 1942 but following the disaster of the Battle of the Barents Sea and the fall of Grossadmiral Raeder, a *Führer Befehl* ordered all work ceased on 30 January 1943, the same order that curtailed work once and for all on *Graf Zeppelin* as the complexion of Germany's naval war, and indeed its command hierarchy, had changed dramatically.

Similar but not identical in size, the two *Jade*-class ship hulls were constructed entirely of welded steel, with 12 watertight compartments and a double bottom. A crew of 79 officers and 804 men was planned for *Jade*, including 134 pilots and technical personnel supplied by the Luftwaffe. Precise data for the *Elbe* does not exist, but it is estimated that its crew would have been similar. The *Jade* was powered by a pair of Deschimag steam turbines, each serving a three-blade propeller and with steam supplied by four

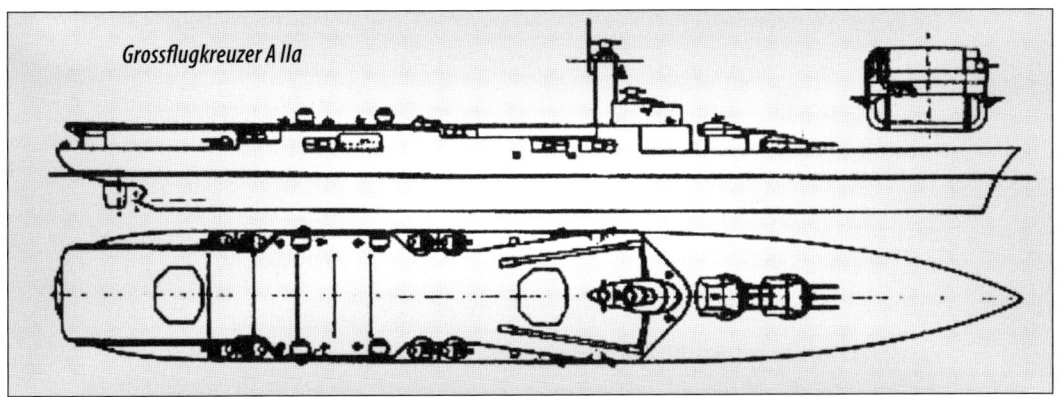

Grossflugkreuzer: A battleship-sized version of the *Flugdeckkrezuer*.

high-pressure boilers. The *Elbe* instead had two electric motors, each served by two turbo-generators, driving two four-blade propeller shafts. Both ships, despite the different engines, could travel at a maximum speed of 21 knots, corresponding to a power of 26,000 hp, but in service they maintained a speed not exceeding 19 knots, at which they had a range of 9,000 nautical miles. This modest speed would have made cooperation with the larger Kriegsmarine warships extremely difficult.

Both ships were to have major anti-aircraft batteries installed. The main battery was made up of eight 105-mm SK C/33 guns, on twin LC/31 mounts, the same originally used for the 88-mm SK C/31 guns very common on Kriegsmarine vessels. This type of triaxial stabilisation support allowed elevation of up to 80°, corresponding to a maximum target altitude of 17,700 metres. Each gun had 3,200 rounds, split between armour-piercing, incendiary and tracer. For close-range aerial targets, defence was entrusted to twelve 37-mm SK C/30 cannon and either twenty-four or thirty-two 20-mm FlaK 38s. Ammunition for the 37-mm numbered 20,000 rounds; the smaller guns were stocked with an overall reserve of 48,000 rounds. The flight deck was planned to be 186 metres long and 27 metres wide, and this class of carrier also featured a single hangar, 148 metres long and 18 metres wide to accommodate the expected twelve Bf 109T and twelve Ju 87E aircraft expected to make up the flight contingent.

Seydlitz, renamed *Weser*, underwent considerable modification with approximately 2,400 tons of material removed from the ship. It was planned to carry ten Bf 109 fighters and ten Ju 87 dive-bombers, maintaining a strong anti-aircraft defence of ten 105-mm SK C/33 guns in twin mounts, ten 37-mm SK C/30 guns in twin mounts, and twenty-four 20-mm Flak 38 guns in *Vierling* mounts. Work on *Seydlitz/Weser* was definitively halted in June 1943, and the hulk towed to Königsberg where it would remain until the war's end and capture by Red Army troops. The *Europa* was captured and requisitioned by the US Army for use as a troop transport unit (named *AP 177*) before transfer to the French government and repurposing back to commercial use. With the abandonment of the conversion project, the *Gneisenau* returned to service as a troop transport, but sank on 2 May 1943, after hitting a mine in the Baltic near the Danish port of Gedser. *Potsdam*, on the other hand, spent the remaining years of the conflict as a barracks ship in Gotenhafen. On 20 June 1946, it passed to the Royal Navy in war reparations and served as a troop carrier under the name of *Empire Fowey* before being sold to Pakistan, who kept it in service under the name *Safina-E-Hujjaj* until the ship was finally scrapped in 1976. *De Grasse* was returned to France after the war and was finally completed in the 1950s to a revised anti-aircraft cruiser design.

PART IV

Smaller Surface Vessels

Explosive Motorboats: *Linsen*

With the creation of the *Kleinkampfverbände*, various weapon systems were developed which required extremely high-risk missions for their crew. However, as stated previously, unlike their Axis partner Japan, neither Italy nor Germany seriously considered out-and-out suicide weapons as a viable combat method. Despite the fact that 'total commitment' was at various times asked of conventional U-boat crews and Luftwaffe fighter pilots (Sonderkommando *Elbe* was formed with the intention of ramming enemy bombers) German authorities never *specifically* required human sacrifices, although the missions were tantamount to suicidal.

Among the naval weapons employed by Germany that resembled an equivalent Japanese type was the *Linse* (Lentil) explosive motorboat. Instead of any relation to the Japanese *Shinyo* suicide weapon (used from August 1944), these were actually inspired by experiences using such weapons during the First World War when the Germans had deployed *Fernlenkboote*. Also relevant was the more contemporary Italian *Motoscafo da Turismo Modificato* project (MTM), whose history is summarised below for clarity and completeness.

In 1935, while Italy was at war with Ethiopia and the Royal Navy posed a potential threat to essential logistical supply lines that trailed across the Mediterranean, the Prince Amedeo, Duke of Aosta, an officer in the Regia Aeronautica, and his brother Prince Aimone, at that time Duke of Spoleta, of the Regia Marina, devised between them a new weapon system that would be quick to construct and simple to use. This novel weapon required the commitment of

Naval presentation to assembled dignitaries (including Albert Speer and Adolf Galland) of a *Linsen* explosive motor boat.

both their service arms: it was a motorboat (*barchino*) loaded with explosives in the bow and piloted by a single man that was capable of being transported to within range of its target by a Savoia-Marchetti S.55 seaplane.

The idea received considerable attention from its inception and was the subject of very positive experiments. However, changes in Italy's international situation diminished interest in such explosive boats until the end of 1938, when they were taken under consideration by a new research and development section of the Plans Office of the Italian General Staff, which tasked the 1st MAS (*Motoscafo armato silurante*, torpedo-armed motorboat) Flotilla at La Spezia with resuming experiments. On 29 September 1938 a proposal for the purchase of twelve new motorboats was submitted to the Minister of the Navy. From evaluation tests of these first models, shipyards were asked to create a prototype which was subsequently assigned the acronym MTM (*Motoscafo da Turismo Modificato*, or, Modified Touring Motorboat), 5.4 metres long at the waterline (6.15 metres overall), with an accentuated V-shaped bow area in order to obtain maximum seaworthiness and course stability.

In this new prototype the engine was equipped with an inverter and upgraded to allow three hours of autonomous travel at maximum speed. In addition, the positions of the triggers for the main charge were designed to increase safety and ease of use and the secondary charges, which were used to destroy the hull, were equipped with an electric trigger. The MTM small boats also experimented with a pilot position as comfortable and dry as possible, generally with the pilot sitting overhanging the stern on a cantilevered transom which tilted to facilitate abandoning the boat. A single example was used for tests at the seaplane base at Milan from 1 March 1941, but using an engine that had been recovered from a previous boat that had exploded on its own test. During the trials, the MTM reached a speed of 33 knots but, above all, it demonstrated the stability

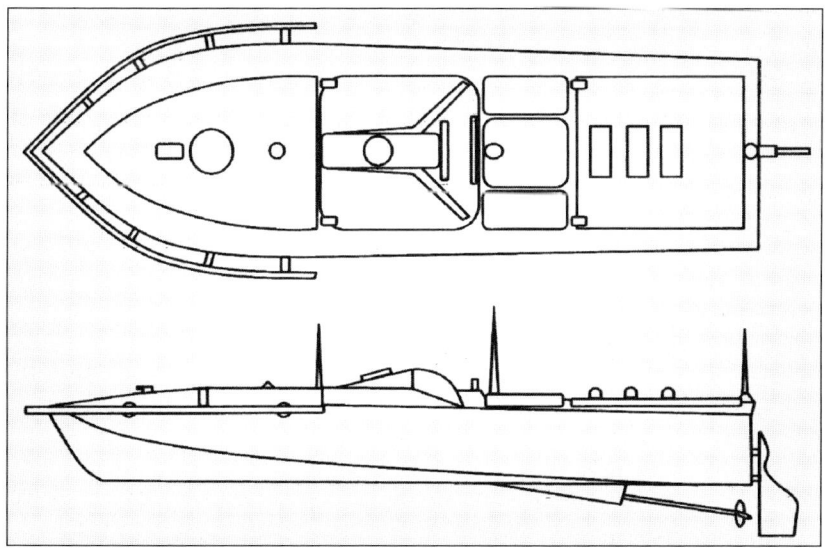

General arrangement of the *Linsen* craft.

> **Linsen Technical Details**
>
> Displacement: 1.2–1.8 tons
> Dimensions: length 5.75–6.15 metres; beam 1.7 metres; average draft 0.45 metres
> Engine: 90-hp 6-cylinder Alfa-Romeo 2500, or 95-hp Ford V-8
> Speed: 31 knots (57 km/h)
> Range: 85 naut. miles @ 31 knots
> Crew: 1
> Armament: 300- or 400-kg depth charge, 7 small scuttling charges

required for effective handling in action. The definitive profile of the MTM became a waterline hull length 5.38 metres (overall 6.11 metres), beam of 1.66 metres, height 1.04 metres and a total weight of 1,200 kg.

There was another variant of the explosive motor boat constructed to different specifications because it came from the SIAI-Marchetti shipyard in Sesto Calende. These were called MTM-D or MTM-M1, built to fill a Kriegsmarine order of 170 vessels. However, 143 of them passed to the Republican version of the famous 10th MAS Flotilla, 'Decima-MAS', that re-formed and stayed loyal to Mussolini's fascist government after the armistice of September 1943, under the command of Prince Junio Valerio Borghese. This version adopted a shell construction, not planking, through the process of quickly working hot materials starting from aeronautical – and therefore hydrodynamic – shapes, obtaining a hull built in less time and requiring less reinforcement. Waterproofing was also handled differently, through the application of synthetic resin and layers of canvas of the type used in aircraft skins. The resultant small boats built using these methods were appreciably heavier.

The use of explosive motorboats by the Wehrmacht did not actually begin with the *Kleinkampfverbände* but rather with the organisation which eventually triggered their formation. The Abwehr had established the commando units that became known as the Brandenburger Regiment at the war's beginning. This gradually morphed into a sprawling conventional Panzergrenadier division, but in early 1942 its Light Engineer Company had begun transforming into a seaborne raiding unit under the command of Hauptmann Max Horlbeck and then Oberleutnant Herbert Kriegsheim. The complement of an officer, 26 NCOs and 163 men transferred to the naval training vessel *Gorch Fock* in Swinemünde, remaining under the command of Abwehr Abteilung II as an independent component of the Brandenburger Regiment. The Kriegsmarine operated its own amphibious units that would later evolve into naval infantry and the *Kleinkampfverbände*. The majority of Kriegsheim's unit eventually moved to Odessa once their time aboard the *Gorch Fock* was over, rebased later at Nikolayev to complete their training on the Black Sea coast from where they would eventually mount their first combat operations. By late 1942 the company had relocated to Langenargen on Lake Constance where it was officially designated as Küstenjäger

An assault boat demonstrates its ability to clear an obstacle.

Abteilung z.b.V. 800 'Brandenburg', was now at roughly battalion strength and an equivalent of the British Special Boat Service. The *Abteilung* comprised a headquarters, two companies equipped with Type 41 *Pionierlandungsboote* (Engineer Landing Craft) and Type 42 *Sturmbooten* (Storm Boats), a third with former French private motor yachts and the 4th (Heavy) Company equipped with twelve *Linsen* explosive motor boats and two control boats, as well as a small group of trainee frogmen; these last would later be grouped together as the Meeresjäger Abteilung 'Brandenburg' in 1943. They also operated a number of small torpedo boats (*Schneiderboote*).

The Küstenjäger Abteilung command passed to the one-legged Rittmeister Conrad von Leipzig and in January 1943 the 4th (Heavy) Company numbered two craft of the Italian X Flotilla MAS Borghese, six heavy Sturmboote 42 and twelve *Linsen* explosive motorboats with one light machine gun and various flak weapons.

The mission brief for the Küstenjäger Abteilung revolved around anti-partisan operations at sea and missions behind enemy lines against harbours and shipping. Parts of the 4th (Heavy) Company were also deployed in Italy during this period. They and the *Linsen* explosive motorboats that they had been designing and testing on Lake Constance, were finally entrained for the front line and a planned operation against the accumulated Allied shipping off Anzio beach. They set out by train on 24 March 1944 and were originally due to be used in support of a *Neger* attack planned by the Kriegsmarine's *Kleinkampfverbände*. However, following cancellation of the *Neger* deployment, the Küstenjäger finally went it alone on 1 July, launching from La Spezia and heading into the Golfo di Genova. There, the deficiencies of the little craft were fully revealed as the light spruce hulls were virtually unmanageable in rough sea conditions as opposed to the calm lake in which they had trained. The mission was a disaster and never came close to the enemy. Vizeadmiral Helmuth Heye, head of the *Kleinkampfverbände*, furiously demanded that naval operations be left to his Kriegsmarine and the explosive motorboats were transferred to his command. Members of the 4th Company were presented with a choice:

Several moored *Linsen*. The idea of converting touring motorboats to different types of military uses was mainly due to the Regia Marina, whose MTM motorboats were purchased by the Kriegsmarine and German versions modelled on them.

return to the Küstenjäger for redeployment under the command of their popular 'Conny' von Leipzig, or join the Kriegsmarine. The company divided itself: many of the men had been involved with the development of the little craft under Brandenburg Major Golbach and harboured a desire finally to use them in action, even if it meant leaving the division. At any rate, by the time that they made their decision to stay or leave, the Brandenburg Division had undergone its final and dramatic metamorphosis.

Further improvements to the design of the MTM were requested by both the Germans and the Italian Social Republic during 1944, but they did not advance beyond the drawing board. The *Linsen* did not conform to a single configuration, and those employed in the Mediterranean were mostly of the SIAI-Marchetti M.1 or Cabi-

Linsen pilots board their explosive boats. The rubber suit worn by pilots is obvious in this photograph.

Cattaneo MTM-D type, ordered by the Kriegsmarine from the Italian manufacturers. Powered by an 87-hp Alfa-Romeo 6C 2500 engine, they reached a speed of 32 knots (59 km/h) and carried an explosive charge of 300 kg. There is conflicting information regarding the number of small boats that the Kriegsmarine possessed; only the aforementioned order for 170 is precisely documented, although some sources suggest that the Germans may have purchased as many as 1,200 vessels.

Having found the light spruce hulls of the Italian boats too delicate and unstable during operational use, the Kriegsmarine implemented a crash building programme of its own during 1944 under the guidance of ObltzS F. H. Wendel, the leader of the *Kleinkampfverbände*'s Construction and Testing department. His new *Linsen* were manufactured originally by Königsberg's Empacher & Kalisch boatbuilders before being farmed out to other building yards and displaced a loaded maximum of 1.85 tons, height of only 80 cm and had a length of 5.75 metres. Powered by a 3.6-litre V8 Ford-Otto engine, giving 95 hp and turning two contra-rotating propellers, the design was able to reach a maximum of 33 knots; cruising endurance was rated at 100 nautical miles at a speed of 15 knots. Two 5-litre containers were carried which could lay a dense smokescreen as a boat attacked; the 'warhead' was a hydrostatic depth charge of between 300 and 400 kg of high explosive stored in the stern. Its trigger was generally a metal framework fitted around the bow of the craft, kept 15 cm away from the gunwale by springs. If compressed, the frame touched the metal of the gunwale and completed a circuit to detonate a small charge held in the bow. Some used instead a single bow-mounted lever that would activate the explosives once depressed. By either method, the initial contact would activate seven small scuttling charges and blow the bow off, allowing the hull to sink, after which the hydrostatic depth charge would explode at a depth of three to five metres, using the magnifying effect of the underwater pressure wave to cause the greatest possible damage to the target hull.

Each *Linsen* unit consisted of a *Rotte* of boats (led by a *Rottenführer*), and made up of a control vessel and two explosive boats. The control boat carried three men, a pilot and two radio men who would each operate the remote control for an explosive boat. These were piloted by a single man who, when close enough to the target, would set the boat to high speed and switch the controls from manual to remote as well as activating two navigation lights visible from astern, one green at the bow and one red at the stern. The remote-control operator could then judge the course of the boat by aligning the two lights using a small control box on his lap with six navigational settings – starboard, port, start engine, stop engine, accelerate, decelerate – and a final firing switch either to scuttle the craft or if manual activation was otherwise deemed necessary. Once engaged on its final attack run, the pilot – wearing a rubber self-inflating life suit – would bail out, hopefully to be collected by the control boat after its remote-control guidance had completed the attack. The remote-control technology used was of two types, the first being derived from the Borgward IV ground demolition vehicle, which was applied to no more than 200 units, and the other a 'wire guide' such as that used by *Goliath* mini demolition vehicles.

Eventually the *Kleinkampfverbände* assembled eleven flotillas of *Linsen*, under the umbrella of Kapitänleutnant Helmut Bastian's Lehrkommando 200. The initial cadre assembled in June 1944 from the assortment of mixed Kriegsmarine and Brandenburg men that had trained alongside Italians of Decima Mas at Sesto Calende. Each flotilla was intended to be comprised of 32 explosive and 16 control boats.

The inaugural operation for the Linsen took place, not as expected in Italy, but off the Normandy beachhead in June 1944. Oberleutnant Helmut Plikat led 211th K-Flotilla to Le Havre on 19 June where they were quartered in a luxurious villa that had belonged to the Rothschild family. In total they mustered twenty-four *Linsen* as well as ancillary units for communication, logistics and even a small antiaircraft detachment. The boats would operate from Hornfleur and it was there that they were finally put into the water on the evening of 25 June: eight control and nine explosive boats were towed to sea by *Räumboote* (motor minesweepers) of the 4th R-Flotilla from Boulogne. Unfortunately, although the commanders and crew of the nimble R-boats were experienced veterans, the same was not true of their charges and as *R-46* eased from port, its towed explosive *Linse* was mishandled by its young pilot and struck the R-boat, closing the circuit and exploding its charge, sinking both vessels as well as two control *Linsen* and another explosive one. As shock waves buffeted the remainder, towlines became entangled and the operation was scrubbed, while the survivors all returned to port. Two further attempts during June ended in similar circumstances, until the entire flotilla was pulled out as unserviceable.

On 2 August the re-formed flotilla sent 16 control and 28 explosive *Linsen* on another mission alongside the *Marders* of 362nd K-Flotilla and *Negers* of 361st K-Flotilla from Villers-sur-Mer. This time the majority of boats set out successfully, though due to deteriorating

Above: a *Kobra* motorboat, a derivative of the *Linsen*, apparently on fire after being abandoned by the pilot but the circumstances under which this photograph was taken are unknown.

weather four control and eight explosive boats were unable to launch. Only ten control *Linsen* returned, seven of which each reported one explosive boat scuttled due to technical failure. However, in return they claimed to have destroyed, in conjunction with the manned torpedoes, between 40,000 and 50,000 tons of enemy shipping. In reality, the piloted torpedoes sank the destroyer HMS *Quorn* while *Linsen* sank the minesweeping trawler HMS *Gairsay*, hit by a single boat, and *LCG 764* rammed by two boats simultaneously.

Another mission on 9 August saw twelve control and sixteen explosive boats leave the Dives estuary, four of the control boats failing to return, but claimed a destroyer, escort vessel, LST and six merchant ships hit. Though Allied records do not corroborate any of this, Leutnant Alfred Vettner, a group leader of the flotilla, was awarded the Knight's Cross on 12 August.

During that month there remained in Italy a mixed bag of Italian and German explosive motorboats operating under the banner of the Decima Mas. At the end of the month the German contingent were designated as Einsatzstab *Haun* under the command of Korvettenkapitän Kurt Haun, moving to Villefranche to operate

Instrument panel of the *Linse* captured intact by USS *Gleaves*.

against shipping near Nice. The unit numbered approximately a hundred Germans of Lehrkommando 600 as well as fifty additional Italians. From there they reported carrying out several successful attacks, although Allied records do not confirm this. From Villefranche they relocated to San Remo where Kapitänleutnant Wilhelm Ulrich assumed command of what was known thereafter as 611th K-Flotilla. As the unit rested and regrouped, Ullrich attended a mass Hitler Jugend rally at which Dönitz was also present to encourage naval recruitment. Reichsjugendleiter Artur Axmann subsequently bestowed on the *Linsen* flotilla the honorific 'Hitler Jugend' title, an armband similar to that issued to the 12th SS Panzer Division being given to the flotilla's members.

At about 0300 hrs on 2 October at least four *Linsen* attacked the American destroyer USS *Gleaves* which engaged the craft with gunfire; two were seen to self destruct as they were turned in pursuit, before the destroyer departed unscathed. Returning after daylight *Gleaves* recovered an abandoned liferaft and disabled boat (marked '8-B') with two Germans aboard; 23-year-old Matrose Karl Heinz Senff and 25-year-old Matrose Hermann Schurring.* The operator, Senff, claimed that engine trouble had prevented either a successful attack or escape. The two Germans present an interesting example of *Kleinkampfverbände* volunteers:

---

* This boat could be the one that, after the war, became part of the collection of the De Henriquez museum in Trieste.

Prisoners of war taken aboard USS *Gleaves* following an abortive *Linsen* attack.

[Schurring] entered the Army in 1937 from a technical school ... He was in the infantry, was wounded in Russia, returned to duty, and again wounded by stepping on a field mine before Leningrad. This disabled him for further Infantry service and he was placed in a supply unit in the back areas. From this station, he, having got tired of it, volunteered for the widely advertised solo fighter service and entered the Navy for this duty in May 1944 ... [Senff]'s story as to origin and entry into the service is about the same as the other. He entered the Navy for the solo fighter service in May of this year, having already served since 1940 in the Army in various units, ranging from infantry to tank units and recruiting service . . . He was a landsman, no sea experience, took a training course in the summer and probably arrived in this area the same time as the others, namely, in August.*

Retaliation was heavy, aided by intelligence from the boat itself, both prisoner interrogation and the fact that the Enigma net used by the *Kleinkampfverbände* – 'Eichendorff', known as 'Bonito' to Allied cryptanalysts – had been broken and was being read consistently from July 1944, only two months since its first use. On 20 October, still in the waters of the Ligurian Riviera di Ponente, a shore bombardment by the French destroyer *Forbin* struck the area of the flower market in Corsini, temporarily used to store the explosive boats. This destroyed forty-eight *Linsen* and four MTM. Despite this, three nights later, the largest number of assault boats ever deployed launched an attack on ships in the Gulf of Juan. This proved futile: eleven of twenty German boats failed to return and the backbone of the *Linsen* formations in the Mediterranean was broken, a setback from which they never truly recovered.

Linsen were used against bridges and pontoon bridges on the Eastern Front and plans were even made to deliver one to attack British ships in Scapa Flow via a Gotha Go 242 glider, though this never advanced beyond this – irrational – idea. Perhaps the most difficult raid to reconstruct is the assault carried out against the port of Livorno by the 611th K-Flotilla in April 1945 in amongst attacks by splintered *Kleinkampfverbände* units still active in the Adriatic, including frogmen, assault boats and *Linsen*. The most probable explanation is that the young volunteers of this formation still had five torpedo motorboats and eleven or twelve explosive boats, all of Italian construction. The strategically important port of Livorno had already been the target of several attacks by both German and

---

* 'Report of Explosive Boat Attack on USS Gleaves', US Eighth Fleet, File No. A16-3, 19 October 1944. https://www.fold3.com/image/292548047.

Italian fascist units and in response had been equipped with a Zebra radar installation to enhance its defence.

Between 0245 and 0330 hrs the approaching 'V-formation' of 611th K-Flotilla boats, which had set sail five hours before from Portofino, was detected and recognised as hostile. Subjected to a heavy bombardment by coastal batteries, the pilots abandoned the boats and the attempt misfired completely. Similar operations were also carried out by the 612th K-Flotilla that was divided into two sub-units based in Portoroz and on the island of Brijuni, and had a total of sixteen small boats – a mixture of *Linsen*, MTM and other Italian variants. It is interesting to note that the *Kleinkampfverbände* also carried out some attacks by transporting raiders on MTSM motorboats to a spot close to their target, before they were shipped in canoes equipped with explosive charges. Among the numerous operations carried out by this special unit, the one against Split on 11 February 1945 was conducted with five *Linsen* and a support boat. The potential targets present in the port were the British cruiser HMS *Dehli* and an LCT-3 that had been converted into a floating gunboat.

After leaving the Istrian coast shortly before midnight, near the island of Drvenik the support boat malfunctioned, and additional fuel stored on board was distributed among the remaining vessels still operational and the boat quietly scuttled. The remainder of the inbound journey took longer than expected and while the attackers were near the island of Brac they could already see the port of Split in the pre-dawn light. The Germans did not respond to signals from a Partisan look-out and as a result came under light-weapons fire, though to no effect. By this stage it was 0545 hrs, only an hour and a quarter before dawn, but the cloudy sky convinced the attackers that the risk of them being sighted remained low. The harbour barriers had been left open due to exiting patrol boats; the Allies in any case considered that the danger of a German assault in the area was minimal. While near the first defensive shore battery, Punta Sustjepan, the leading elements of 612th K-Flotilla took another barrage of light-weapons fire and ignored further requests to

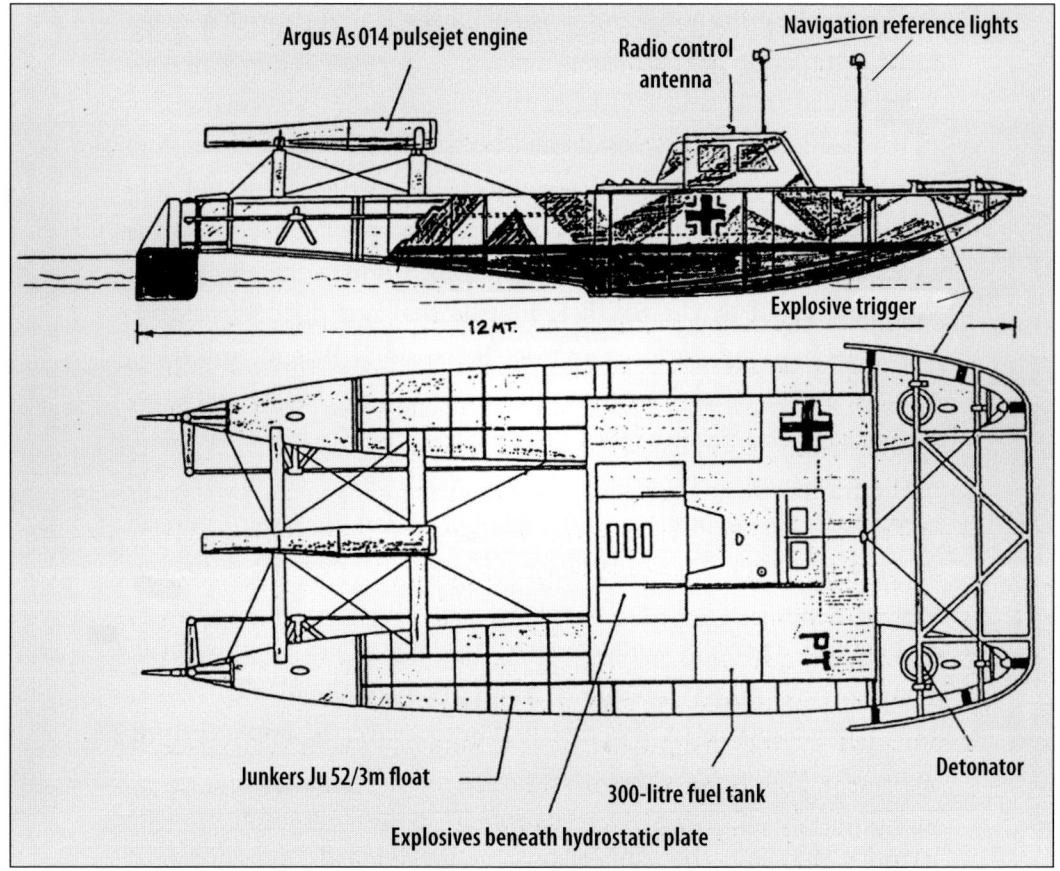

Drawings that reconstruct the possible appearance of the Sprengboot *Tornado*, designed by Engineer Grochalsky. A prototype was tested but was scuttled in 1945.

identify themselves. The Yugoslav defenders then lit up a searchlight, blinding some pilots and sending one of the small boats crashing into the breakwater. The light also illuminated *Dehli* and the final attack began. One boat was stopped by machine-gun fire; another headed directly towards the cruiser until at the last moment, perhaps due to a current, it deflected towards the LCT floating battery and exploded, severely damaging it and causing some damage also to *Dehli*'s stern and rudder. The last boat attempted to retreat but was intercepted. The episode was considered a success by the Kriegsmarine, while for the Allies it remained somewhat obscure as Yugoslav authorities minimised the incident in order not to take responsibility for the ineffectiveness of their defence.

Explosive Motorboat *Tornado*

The availability of the Argus As 014 pulsejet engine that was used as propulsion for the Fieseler Fi 103 V-1 'flying bomb', prompted an engineer by the name of Grochalsky at the end of 1944 to submit to the Kriegsmarine a project for the experimental use of this engine on a small boat. Named the 'Tornado', this would have been an explosive small boat built by reusing two floats produced for the trimotor Junkers Ju 52/3m transport aircraft in its seaplane configuration. A first test took place in the Baltic Sea, near the town of Travemünde. For this test, the pulsejet engine was mounted on a single float, with the result that the boat immediately careered out of control, demonstrating that it did not possess the stability necessary to maintain a set course and in fact even reversing direction during the unsuccessful trial. Instead, under the more controlled conditions provided by the hydrodynamic test tank at the HSVA research institute in Hamburg, a version with two parallel hulls in a catamaran configuration was successfully trialled.

The last test cycle was carried out near the place of origin of the Argus pulsejet, the famous rocket test site of Peenemünde, in the Baltic waters off the island of Usedom. There the experimental boat reached a speed of 48 knots in calm sea conditions though it was difficult to control at higher speeds. It was successfully radio-controlled and wire-guided by a control boat operating close to the target with the sighting help of the same stern-facing navigation lights as had been fitted aboard *Linsen*. In the scarce literature existing on this vehicle there

Above: a reconstruction of the *Tornado*, with the Argus pulsejet.

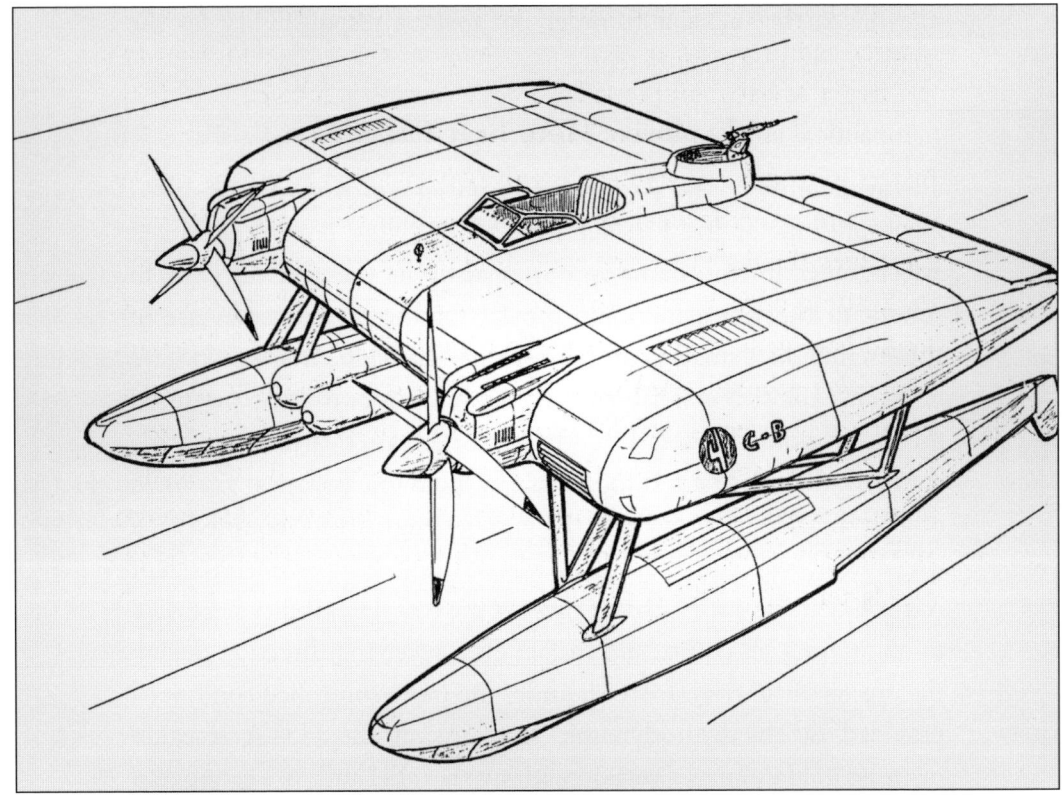

The Italian Caproni Type B project had similarities to the *Tornado* design.

are indications of armament consisting of explosive charges in the floats near the waterline, for a potential total weight of 700 kg of high explosive, fitted with the same hydrostatic triggers used in the *Linsen*. Harrauer speculated that they were devices derived from Luftwaffe components – like most of this vehicle – but also that the *Tornado* could be used with towed explosive arrays as an effective tool against port barriers, or alternatively for the delivery of frogmen. Regardless, none of these principles was ever applied as the prototype of the *Tornado* was sunk in Peenemünde as the area risked capture by advancing Soviet troops.

Harrauer's research on this *Sprengboot* uncovered a similarity with an Italian project of the 1930s, attributed to Engineer Gianni Caproni, and previously described in literature only by the historian

Achille Rastelli. It seems that the designers from Milan's Taliedo quarter had proposed at least three designs of fast torpedo boats to the Regia Marina, all propelled by the Isotta-Fraschini Asso 1000 aeronautical engine. One of them, Type B, of two parallel floats 10 metres in length and equipped with two thrusters operating quad-blade aircraft propellers, was capable of carrying two 450-mm torpedoes thanks to a wing section of 7 metres, with ailerons on the trailing edge for buoyancy control. The two 1,000-hp engines would have generated a surface effect similar to that of the Russian *ekranoplan* – the so-called 'Ground Effect Vehicle' – pushing the craft at a speed between 65 and 80 knots, but only in sea conditions below force 3. It is assumed that these plans never advanced beyond the drawing stage, their noteworthy aspect remaining their modernity and the way in which they perhaps rekindled widespread interest in ever faster torpedo boats during the 1930s.

PART V

Landing Wonder Weapons

Amphibious and Coastal Armaments

Though outside of the remit of Kriegsmarine weapons, these maritime aspects of other service vehicles warrant inclusion for their potential role in amphibious operations.

Tauchpanzer

The Tauchpanzer III was a genuine German secret weapon, not a simple amphibious version of the PzKpfw III but a completely submersible variant. Although Hitler understood that the invasion of Great Britain was a major amphibious operation, he somewhat naively thought of it more in terms akin to an 'extended river crossing' than a full scale invasion from the sea. Codenamed *Unternehmen Seelöwe* (Operation Sealion) the attack was originally vaguely intended for September 1940 once the Luftwaffe had neutralised the threat posed by the Royal Air Force. Aside from a few *Fallschirmjäger* drops a massive deployment of ground forces under the command of Generalfeldmarschall Gerd von Rundstedt was to undertake the invasion, carried across the English Channel in a manner indeed more befitting a large river crossing. They largely intended to use improvised barges as the purpose-designed *Marinefährprähme* was some time in the future, in actual fact designed as a result of this abortive invasion plan.

The Kriegsmarine was not suited to such an ambitious invasion, as had been evidenced by the catastrophic losses suffered during the invasion of Norway and in the subsequent support of troops ashore in the face of effective Royal Navy retaliation. Notwithstanding the

A *Schwimmpanzer* (*top*) aboard its transport vessel, and (*above*) fully afloat.

A Schwimmpanzer III drops into the water from its landing barge during preparations for Operation Sealion . . .

problems posed for the Channel crossing by the formidable British naval forces, the river barges collected for use during this massive operation would have proved unsuitable and too vulnerable to the sea conditions alone, on all but the calmest of days.

Nevertheless, the Wehrmacht began equipping some improvised transport vessels with engines, planning to have a fleet of 800 self-propelled rafts out of the 2,400 available in Germany, France, Holland and Belgium. Others still were modified to facilitate speedier landing of infantrymen or to transport submersible tanks or amphibious vehicles. The Wehrmacht also finally created a dedicated landing craft with the Pionierlandungsboot 39 which entered service in September 1940. The 15 metre long and 4.7 metres wide hull could be dismantled into two longitudinal halves for rail transport.

and having made its way underwater to the beach begins to head inland, pulling its 'breathing' hose with its float behind it.

Powered by two 86-hp diesel engines, the shallow draft vessel could reach a speed of 8 knots (15 km/h), was crewed by seven men and had a dead weight of 20 tons, and could carry 10 tons of cargo in weather up to sea state 4. The Pionierlandungsboot 39 was later superseded by improved versions, numerically suffixed '40' and '41', each with gradual increases in size and capacity, until '43' and '45' increased dimensions dramatically and were never put into production. The three original types served predominantly in the Mediterranean and in support of the Eastern Front.

Another vehicle modification sparked by the requirements of Operation Sealion was the Schwimmpanzer II. This was an adapted version of the Panzer II light tank which, with its weight of only 8.9 tons, was light enough to be launched from a specially modified barge

A Panzer III *Tauchpanzer* is lowered into the water during a waterproofing test in the summer of 1940. The cradles to support its snorkel hose have been fitted but the hose itself does not seem to have been installed.

or ferry and float with the attachment of two rectangular aluminium boxes on each side of the hull, filled with bags of kapok for buoyancy. An inflatable rubber ring was mounted between the hull and turret to make the tank watertight and both its main 20-mm cannon and coaxial machine gun were capable of being firing while the vehicle was in the water. Propulsion was handled by the tank's own tracks, connected by axles to a transmission shaft that passed through each float and set two propellers in motion. The Schwimmpanzer II could reach 3 knots (5.7 km/h). Fifty-two of these tanks were prepared before Sealion was cancelled.

While the Schwimmpanzer, and the later highly successful Schwimmwagen scout car, were floating vehicles, the concept behind properly submersible armoured vehicles was relatively simple and mirrored some of the principles later adopted for the ventilation of U-boats. The vehicles were made watertight with the application of special seals of masking tape, rubber and cable tar along all the armour joints; an inflatable rubber ring sealed the join between turret and hull. Those areas into which water could ingress – such as cannon, machine guns, the commander's cupola – were protected by rubber sheaths which, through the use of small pyrotechnic devices, could be blown off once the vehicle emerged from the water, making it immediately combat ready. Air intakes to the engine compartment were completely closed and exhaust pipes were protected by high-pressure, non-return valves; all internal fan gear was disengaged. While submerged, seawater was used to cool the engine and any

During sea trials in August 1940. The *Tauchpanzer* is being lowered by crane into the water, the graduated uprights providing test depth measurement. Trailing from the turret is the flexible air intake tube with the attached flotation buoy out of shot.

> **Tauchpanzer Panzer III (U) Ausf. F Technical Details**
>
> | | |
> |---|---|
> | Weight: | 23 tonnes |
> | Dimensions: | length 5.56 metres; width 2.9 metres; height 2.5 metres |
> | Engine: | 296-hp Maybach 12-cylinder HL 120TR; fuel capacity 300–320 litres |
> | Performance: | maximum road speed 40 km/h, off-road 18–20 km/h |
> | Range: | on road 155 km, off road 95 km; consumption 206 litres/100 km (0.67 km/litre) |
> | Crew: | 5 (commander, driver, radio operator, gunner, loader) |
> | Armament: | 50-mm KwK 38 L/42 main gun; coaxial 7.92-mm MG34; hull mounted 7.92mm MG34 with 3,750 rounds |

seepage removed by use of a bilge pump. The crucial component of the system was a flexible rubber tube, acting as a snorkel, 20 cm in diameter and 18 metres long, connected to a float. The vehicle's radio aerial was also threaded through this tube and by this method the vehicle could be guided by radio – though it also carried a gyroscope for navigation – while travelling submerged to an optimal depth of 8 or 10 metres and maximum of 15 metres. All the crew members were also equipped with Tauchretter, the escape equipment provided for U-boat men. Capable of travelling at a speed of about 5 km/h for 30 minutes, theoretically the vehicle could travel about 2.5 km underwater. The initial experiment with a modified Pzkpfw III Ausf E embarked on the merchant ship *Hans Herbert* took place in August 1940. The submersible tanks were to be launched from converted river barges, sliding into the water along an elongated ramp made of iron rails.

For Sealion four battalions (designated A–D) of submersible panzers were deployed in Armeegruppe A: three battalions attached to Generaloberst Ernst Busch's Sixteenth Army and one to General der Artillerie Christian Hansen's Ninth Army. Between June and October 1940 160 PzKpfw III tanks were converted, generically labelled PzKpfw III (U), the majority being Ausf. E armed with 37-mm cannon and only eight Ausf. F with the improved 50-mm cannon, as well as 42 PzKpfw IV (U), Ausf. D with short barrelled

75-mm main gun. Finally, 8 *Panzerbefehlswagen* III Ausf. E command tanks were also converted and the 52 PzKpfw II (*Schwimm*) were to be spread among the various *Abteilungen*.

Following the suspension of Sealion, the four battalions of *Tauchpanzer* were combined with parts of the 4th and 14th Infantry Divisions to form General der Panzertruppen Walther Nehring's 18th Panzer Division in Chemnitz during October 1940, two battalions forming the 18th Panzer Regiment and two the 28th Panzer Regiment. As part of the general restructuring of Panzer divisions in early 1941, 28th Panzer Regiment was disbanded and one battalion moved to become the 3rd of 18th Panzer Regiment and the other transferred to Generalleutnant Walter Model's 3rd Panzer Division.

As the invasion of the Soviet Union neared – Operation Barbarossa – the *Tauchpanzer* were fitted with rigid snorkels that reached

A submersible *Panzerbefehlswagen* (Command Tank) III Ausf. H(U) of the 18th Panzer Division crossing a river in the Soviet Union, June 1941.

up 3.5 metres in height, replacing the former flexible tubes. Their most prominent action took place at Patulin on the River Bug on 22 June 1941. There the 17th and 18th Panzer Divisions were to cross the river as part of XLVII Panzer Corps, forming the left wing of the German armoured deployment north of Brest-Litovsk. Since there were no bridges, assault troops and a motorcycle company were ferried across in rubber dinghies and assault boats to form a small bridgehead, though they only possessed light machine guns and anti-tank weapons. As engineers began constructing a pontoon bridge, Oberstleutnant Manfred Graf Strachwitz led his 1st Battalion into the river, somewhere in the region of eighty panzers eventually crossing the Bug and reinforcing the bridgehead. Ironically, most heavy Soviet forces had already withdrawn, although the *Tauchpanzer* did counter a probe mounted by Russian armoured cars.

Amphibious Tractor (LWS)

For completeness of the discussion, the *Landwasserschlepper*, abbreviated to LWS and literally translated as 'land-water tractor' deserves a mention. An amphibious tracked vehicle conceived in May 1935 by the German Army Weapons Agency (Heereswaffenamt) cannot be called a 'secret weapon' but it was certainly a vehicle rarely seen in action and just as rarely described in print. The vehicle was considered a relatively low developmental priority, being purely logistical with no armour or weapons; the first three prototypes were not completed until the autumn of 1940.

Two design and testing offices were involved in answering the request for creation of a special amphibious tractor, capable of towing a floating trailer carrying up to 18 tons of cargo (equipment or single vehicles). Given the complexity of the project, some of the major German industrial businesses were involved, the main one being Rheinmetall-Borsig of Düsseldorf. The development process was extremely slow, and the tests were conducted exclusively in rivers and lakes. At the end of June 1940, after the victorious French campaign, the possibility of a landing in Great Britain suddenly became concrete and the LWS project received a renewed boost

Amphibious Tractor (LWS)

A *Landwasserschlepper* during beach-landing trials.

of energy as it could, without any doubt, prove very useful for the planned amphibious landings.

At that point, however, Army inspectors, who included General Franz Halder, Army Chief of Staff, criticised the total lack of armour, absence of onboard weapons and the excessive bulk of the floating trailer as well as the absence of a hatch dedicated to accessing and unloading the transported material. The *Landwasserschlepper* was a curious vehicle composed of a flat-bottomed maritime hull coupled to a system of tracks, and surmounted by a small pilot cabin, capable of accommodating a crew of three men. The closed transport compartment was situated behind the cabin, capable of holding up to twenty fully equipped soldiers, and its maritime genesis emphasised by a series of small circular portholes.

Landwasserschlepper Technical Details	
Weight:	13 tons
Dimensions:	total length 8.6 metres; width 3.16 metres; height 3.13 metres
Engine:	Maybach HL 120 TRM V-12 petrol
Performance:	maximum road speed 35 km/h; in water 6.5 knots
Range:	on road 240 km
Crew:	2
Armament:	None

The tracks were mounted on four bogies on each side, each equipped with two wheels and tied to a leaf-spring suspension, with a drive wheel similar to that found on a Panzer II light tank in the conventional front position and the return wheel at the rear. The Maybach HL 120 TRM V-12 petrol engine was housed in a rear compartment behind the main cargo area, delivering 265 hp at 2,800 rpm which, in addition to the tracks, powered two large propellers located beneath the hull in circular internal cavities. The Kässbohrer amphibious trailer was a large quadrangular platform, with high armoured walls and equipped with a retractable tailgate, which was used to load and unload the up to 20 tons of freight being transported. This 'barge' rested on three axles, one front and two rear. Once on land the tractor would tow it to a safe place in which to unload.

Overall, the *Landwasserschlepper* was an imposing vehicle 8.6 metres long, 3.16 metres wide and 3.13 metres high, with a total weight of 13 tons. Its performance in water was still acceptable despite its size. It was able to reach 6.5 knots (12 km/h) and on land a maximum 35 km/h, covering an operational range up to 150 kilometres.

Despite initial negative comments regarding the vehicle's size, an initial series of four *Landwasserschlepper* was still ordered, to be completed by 11 December 1940, though by this deadline the fourth vehicle was still under construction, but would be completed at the end of the month. Meanwhile, a second series of eight units was

The German armed forces did not have many opportunities to conduct amphibious operations and therefore did not develop many amphibious vehicle types; the Rheinmetall-Borsig LWS (*Landwasserschlepper*) was the most widespread.

requested, which were to be built between March and June 1941 at the rate of two vehicles per month. Contemporary documents, however, indicate that by July 1942 the expected pace had not been met and only seven vehicles were operational. Nonetheless, the Army agreed with Rheinmetall-Borsig for a further series of 14 tractors, to be started between July and August 1942 and carried forward until September 1943: it seems that even this last order was never fulfilled. Alternative sources report rather different data: a total to 21 vehicles completed by March 1941.

Originally it was envisioned as a useful vehicle either for river crossing (within a non-contested area due to its lack of defensive armour) or for engineers in the construction of bridging. The three prototypes, however, were attached to Panzer Abteilung 100 (*Fl*),

Rear view of the *Landwasserschlepper*, showing the circular cavities under the hull which held the propellers.

a flamethrowing battalion that had been formed in May 1940, the LWS vehicles attached to the staff company and apparently crewed at least partially by Kriegsmarine men. As part of this battalion they were envisioned to be useful for the initial landings of the postponed Operation Sealion both as an amphibious tractor for unpowered barges and as a supply ferry transport.

Ultimately the LWS was never used in landing operations and only ever produced in small numbers, perhaps no more than two dozen vehicles. The few completed units were used piecemeal mainly on the Eastern Front and at least a single vehicle served in North Africa as part of the 778th Engineer Landing Company. As such it formed part of Kampfgruppe *Hecker* (led by Oberst Hermann-Hans Hecker, Pionier Führer Afrika), which included men of the 13th Brandenburger Company, 33rd and 39th Panzer Jäger

Battalions, 778th Engineer Landing Company and Italian 3rd 'San Marco' Marine Battalion. In support of General Erwin Rommel's Operation Venezia, the May 1942 attack on the Allied Gazala Line positions, the *Kampfgruppe* was to make an amphibious landing behind enemy lines, Rommel's orders for 26 May outlining the Axis attack closed with instructions that: 'On X+1 Kampfgruppe *Hecker* will land at Gabr Si. Hameida to block the Via Balbia around Kilometre 136.'

Hecker's force was to sever the Allies' supply route by landing 30 km east of Tobruk while Rommel's forces attacked the Gazala Line directly. After rehearsal exercises using the *Landwasserschlepper* the troops were embarked on *Marinefahrprähme* and sailed on 28 May under escort by a mixed force of S-boats and R-boats. However, after only a few hours at sea, the operation was cancelled by radio after Allied resistance proved unexpectedly fierce on the Gazala Line, and all boats returned to Derna to unload and Kampfgruppe *Hecker* moved towards Bir Hakeim where they took part in the attack on the fortress there that was held by Free French troops.

In 1944 a new design – the LWS II – was trialled that used the chassis of a Panzer IV medium tank, retaining its defensive armour,

This special amphibious trailer was also developed for use in conjunction with the *Landwasserschlepper*.

but with a flat rear deck and a small raised armoured pilot cabin at the front. This was built in even smaller numbers as the end of the war approached. Two of these second-generation *Landwasserschlepper* could be joined with a floating platform between them to create the

Siebel Ferry Technical Details	
Displacement:	140–170 tons
Dimensions:	total length 32 metres; beam 15 metres; draft 1.5 metres
Engine:	Variable – typically 4 x Ford V-8 300-hp + 2 x BMW 6U 750-hp aircraft engines
Performance:	maximum speed 11 knots
Range:	300 nautical miles
Crew:	11–14
Armament:	Maximum of 4 x 88-mm anti-aircraft guns, 1 x 20-mm *Flakvierling* mount, or 2 x 20-mm Flak 30 guns

Two LWS IIs joined together in catamaran style with a platform between intended to carry an armoured vehicle.

so-called *'Panzerfahre'*, a self-propelled transport platform capable of accommodating heavy loads. However, trials of this idea were cancelled before the end of the year and only two specimens were actually delivered. In May 1945, after the fall of Nazi Germany and the end of the Second World War, a single LWS was captured by British troops and subsequently evaluated in Great Britain.

Siebel Ferry

Preparations for the invasion of Great Britain had starkly highlighted the lack of suitable landing craft, forcing a reliance on hastily converted civilian barges. All Wehrmacht branches were invited to submit proposals for landing craft designs and the Luftwaffe developed the *Siebel Fähre* (Siebel Ferry, named after its creator, aircraft designer and Luftwaffe Oberst Fritz Siebel). Constructed as a catamaran of two bridge-building pontoons, connected by welded steel cross beams, the unit's main propulsion was to be provided by a pair of 75-hp Ford V-8 engines in each pontoon, each paired unit powering a single marine propeller. Two surplus BMW 6U 750-hp aircraft engines with four-bladed propellers were mounted astern of the pontoons for auxiliary propulsion while the cross beams were intended to support a platform for the payload; vehicles were able to mount and dismount via a bow ramp.

Initial testing on a lake near Berlin failed to impress Franz Halder and an assembled group of Army officers: its speed was low, only 4 knots, and its appearance suggested a fragility that would not withstand the rigours of operational use. Despite these misgivings, Siebel continued to modify his design, reducing the 6-metre space between pontoons to 5.5 metres, and overseeing construction of a large waterproofed steel platform covered with wood planking. Not only would this serve as the payload deck but it would also provide longitudinal and lateral strength and extra weight enabling the craft to operate in anything up to sea state 6.

A fresh prototype test was carried out on the Ems River on 31 August 1940 and with the use of only the aircraft engines, the vessel reached a speed of 7 knots (15 km/h) and in September series production began in Antwerp; 25 were built by the month's end.

This original version of the Siebel Ferry motorised raft was powered by two BMW aircraft engines with four-blade aerial propellers and three Ford truck engines driving marine propellers.

A Siebel Ferry under way, clearly being powered by its in-water propellers. During preparations for Operation Sealion the truck engines were regarded as the main means of propulsion; the aircraft engines were to be kept in reserve and only used during the final stages of a beach landing.

Both the Army and Luftwaffe used Siebel ferries which saw action in most theatres in which German troops fought. They proved to be robust and possessing of good seagoing qualities leading to a number being converted into gun platforms for mobile anti-aircraft use. Variations were also built that carried artillery, headquarters facilities and field hospitals.

The Army tended to shy away from the use of aero engines because of aviation-fuel supply problems; the engines were also considered prone to catching fire. They therefore removed the aircraft engines and upgraded the vehicle engines housed inside each pontoon.

Tiger Projekt NM

The 'Tiger Projekt NM' was a completely unconventional plan to use the chassis of a number of Tiger I heavy tanks as a basis for the construction of a mobile coastal artillery emplacement. The concept,

A Siebel Ferry used as an anti-aircraft platform on the Eastern Front.

which never got further than the drawing board – details are held in German Federal Archives, Bundesarchiv RH8-I-2590-K, in the archival section designated 'Army Weapons Office/Department for Special Equipment (WA Prüf 11) and Army Research Institute Peenemünde' – was to join three Tiger hulls by means of an I-beam girder frame measuring approximately 17 metres by 15 metres, similar to that used in ship construction. On top of this would be mounted three turrets that appear not to have originated from the Tiger tank, each equipped with a 128-mm gun. The entire assemblage would then be camouflaged by a wooden 'box' that covered everything except the gun barrels and was painted to resemble a large building. The box was equipped with three sets of large double doors, so at least some traverse and elevation would be possible.

This project never went beyond its 1943 concept design phase and we have no reference to it beyond these original drawings. Though it is not definitively a Kriegsmarine project, this remains the most likely background, although the Army did construct its own coastal batteries as part of the Atlantic Wall. However, the three large gun turrets lacked any form of fire control, therefore requiring an external source, the sort of arrangement naval batteries specialised in. It appears obvious that this was a coastal gun emplacement as it would have been useless in terrestrial warfare. Aside from the impossibility of transporting this leviathan, the disguise of a large building moving across the steppes of the Eastern Front would seem somewhat absurd. The original general drawings and documentation relate to orders from Krupp (design and construction) and Henschel (Tiger hulls and machinery). There also exist thematically similar designs using Tiger hulls and carrying a single 240-mm or 280-mm gun, but these are more likely to be Army concepts equivalent to existing mobile railway guns.

Select Bibliography

Blocksdorf, Helmut, *Das Kommando der Kleinkampfverbände der Kriegsmarine*, Motorbuch Verlag, Stuttgart, 2003

Fock, Harald, *Die Deutschen Schnellboote*, Koehler Verlag, Hamburg, 2001

———, *Marine Kleinkampfmittel*, Koehler Verlag, Hamburg, 1996

Hadeler, Wilhelm, 'The Aircraft Carrier in the German Navy 1934–1945', *American Society of Naval Engineers Journal*, 1956

Hitler, Adolf, *Hitler's Table Talk*, Weidenfeld & Nicolson, 1953

Mallmann-Showell, Jak, *The German Navy Handbook 1939–1945*, Sutton Publishing, 1999

Paterson, Lawrence, *Hitler's Brandenburgers*, Greenhill Books, London, 2018

———, *Steel and Ice*, History Press, Stroud, 2016

———, *Weapons of Desperation*, Greenhill Books, London, 2006

Raeder, Erich, *Grand Admiral*, Da Capo Press, Boston, 2001

Rössler, Eberhard, *The U-Boat*, Naval Institute Press, 1981

US Navy, Office of Intelligence, *Führer Conferences on Matters Dealing with the German Navy*, Washington, 1947 (translated transcripts)